The Year of the Poet VII

October 2020

The Poetry Posse

inner child press, ltd.

The Poetry Posse 2020

Gail Weston Shazor
Shareef Abdur Rasheed
Teresa E. Gallion
hülya n. yılmaz
Kimberly Burnham
Tzemin Ition Tsai
Elizabeth Esguerra Castillo
Jackie Davis Allen
Joe Paire
Caroline 'Ceri' Nazareno
Ashok K. Bhargava
Alicja Maria Kuberska
Swapna Behera
Albert 'Infinite' Carrasco
Eliza Segiet
William S. Peters, Sr.

~ * ~

In order to maintain each poet's authentic voice, this volume has not undergone the scrutiny of editing. Please take time to indulge each contributor for their own creativity and aspirations to convey their uniqueness.

hülya n. yılmaz, Ph.D.
Director of Editing ~
Inner Child Press International

General Information

The Year of the Poet VII
October 2020 Edition

The Poetry Posse

1st Edition : 2020

Publisher Information

1st Edition : Inner Child Press
intouch@innerchildpress.com
www.innerchildpress.com

ISBN-13 : 978-1-952081-31-6 (inner child press, ltd.)

$ 12.99

WHAT WOULD LIFE BE WITHOUT A LITTLE POETRY?

Dedication

This Book is dedicated to

Humanity, Peace & Poetry

the Power of the Pen

can effectuate change!

The Poetry Posse

past, present & future

our Patrons and Readers

the Spirit of our Everlasting Muse

In the darkness of my life
I heard the music
I danced . . .
and the Light appeared
and I dance

Janet P. Caldwell

Table of Contents

The Poetry Posse

Table of Contents . . . *continued*

Foreword

Kim Dae-jung was President of South Korea from 1998 to 2003. He was awarded the Nobel Peace Prize in 2000 for his work for democracy and human rights in South Korea, and for peace and reconciliation with North Korea. He sought to lay the foundation of a peaceful reunification of north and south Korea, which had been in a state of war since 1950 by means of his "sunshine policy" of mutual understanding and friendliness.

Kim Dae-jung was born on 6 January 1924 but had it changed to 3 December 1925 to avoid conscription under Japanese colonial rule. Kim was the second of seven children. There were many attempts to kill him for his opposition to military rulers in South Korea. Kim reflected on these events during his 2000 Nobel Peace Prize lecture:

"I have lived, and continue to live, in the belief that God is always with me. I know this from experience. In August of 1973, while exiled in Japan, I was kidnapped from my hotel room in Tokyo by intelligence agents of the then military government of South Korea. The news of the incident startled the world. The agents took me to their boat at anchor along the seashore. They tied me up, blinded me, and stuffed my mouth. Just when they were about to throw me overboard, Jesus Christ appeared before me with such clarity. I clung to him and begged him to save me. At that very moment, an airplane was sent down from Heavens by the almighty God Himself to rescue me from the moment of death." At the age of 85 Kim died on 18 August 2009.

Kim was a great leader at getting people and nations together. He brought people of India and Korea together by focusing on ancient stories that Princess Suriratna of Ayodhya got married to King Suro of Korea 2,000 years ago. Interestingly, Kim Dae-jung claimed his ancestry to the princess of India. Today, descendants of the couple number more than six million, which is roughly about 10% of the South Korean population.

The tomb of the princess is located in city of Kimhae near Busan. Koreans have also preserved the rocks that are said to have been used by the princess during her sea voyage to Korea to keep her boat stable.

Then in 2001, more than 100 historians and government representatives, including the North Korean ambassador to India, unveiled Queen Suriratna or Hwang-ok's (her Korean name) memorial on the west bank of the River Saryu in Ayodhya.

This story inspired me to author a book of poems titled Mirror of Dreams which was launched by Counsel Generals of Korea and India in Vancouver in 2004.

Ashok K. Bhargava
Founder & President
Writers International Network, Canada

Now Available

www.innerchildpress.com/anthology-free-downloads

Preface

Dear Family and Friends,

Yes I am excited and feel accomplished as we are on the last leg of our seventh year of publishing what I and many others deem to be a worthy enterprise, *The Year of the Poet*.

This year we have aligned our vision with that of Nober Peace Prize Recipients. We have title this year's theme. The Year of Peace! Hopefully thorugh our sharing each month, our poetry can have a profound effect on our global consciousness and the need for peace while educating ourselves and our readership about some of the individuals who have made history through their efforts to promulgate peace for all of humanity.. We are on our way to hitting yet another milestone. Needless to say, I am elated.

To reiterate, our initial vision was to just perform at this level for the year of 2014. Since that time we have had the blessed opportunity to include many other wonderful poets, word artists and storytellers in the Poetry Posse from lands, cultures and persuasions all over the world. We have featured hundreds of additional poets, thereby introducing their poetic offerings to our vast global audience.

In keeping with our effort and vision to expand the awareness of poets from all walks by making this offerings accessible, we at Inner Child Press International will continue to make every volume a FREE Download. The books are also available for purchase at the affordable cost of $7.00 per volume.

In the previous years, our monthly themes were Flowers, Birds, Gemstones, Trees and Past Cultures. This coming year we have elected to continue our focus of choosing what we consider a significant subject . . . PEACE! In each month's volume you will have the opportunity to not only read at least one poem themed by our Poetry Posse members about such celebrated Peace Ambassadors, but we have included a few words about each individual in our prologue. We hope you find the poetic offerings insightful as we use our poetic form to relay to you what we too have learned through our research in making our offering available to you, our readership.

In closing, we would like to thank you for being an integral part of our amazing journey.

Enjoy our amazing featured poets . . . they are amazing!

Building Cultural Bridges of Understanding . . .

Bless Up . . . From the home in our hearts to yours

Bill

The Poetry Posse
Inner Child Press Ineternational

PS

Do Not forget about the World Healing, World Peace Poetry effort.

Available here

www.worldhealingworldpeacepoetry.com

For Free Downloads of Previous Issues of The Year of the Poet

www.innerchildpress.com/the-year-of-the-poet

Kim Dae-jung
2000

Each month for the year of 2020, which we have deemed as *The Year of Peace*, we at Inner Child Press International will be celebrating through our poetry a few Nobel Peace Prize Recipients who have contributed greatly to humanity via their particular avocations. This month of Julu 2020 you will find select poems from each Poetry Posse member on this month's celebrants.

In 2000, The Nobel Peace Prize was awarded to Kim Dae-jung.

For more information about visit :

www.nobelprize.org/prizes/peace/2000/dae-jung/biographical/

https://en.wikipedia.org/wiki/Kim_Dae-jung

www.britannica.com/biography/Kim-Dae-Jung

World Healing, World Peace Foundation

human beings for humanity

worldhealingworldpeacefoundation.org

Poets . . .
sowing seeds in the
Conscious Garden of Life,
that those who have yet to come
may enjoy the Flowers.

Poets, Writers . . . know that we are the enchanting magicians that nourishes the seeds of dreams and thoughts . . . it is our words that entice the hearts and minds of others to believe there is something grand about the possibilities that life has to offer and our words tease it forth into action . . . for you are the Poet, the Writer to whom the Gift of Words has been entrusted . . .

~ wsp

Poetry succeeds where instruction fails.

~ wsp

I
Fly
because
I Can
...said the Dreamer to the world.

Gail Weston Shazor

This is a creative promise ~ my pen will speak to and for the world. Enamored with letters and respectful of their power, I have been writing for most of my life. A mother, daughter, sister and grandmother I give what I have been given, greatfilledly.

Author of . . .

"An Overstanding of an Imperfect Love"
&
Notes from the Blue Roof

Lies My Grandfathers Told Me

available at Inner Child Press.

www.facebook.com/gailwestonshazor
www.innerchildpress.com/gail-weston-shazor
navypoet1@gmail.com

A Day for Peace
(Nonet)

Years

Fifty

North and South

Is now gone away

Winter and summer

And I have longed for you

My sister from the same womb

We live on soil and under sky

Separated by memories of war

Maybe soon I will hold you as before

Lis'n Lis'n

Y'all better listen quick
Somebody trying to learn
You something
It ain't when they got you
That you in trouble
Cause another man done gone
From the county farm
The gate was left just a bit ajar
Just a bit so he could see
And the others said
Nah man
This is protective custody
In here we safe
And they waited for the feeding time
Stuff slid under the door
Thrown over the fence
To keep everyone from roaring
The only bit of lightness
Was the complexion of the hand
They had been trained not to bite
But the door called out
Swinging gently on its rusty hinge
Singing slyly and waiting
Freedom oh freedom
Was its plaintive plea
And he knew the sun actually shone
Beyond this protection
Because he had been there
Free
From the county farm
The chains had been left long enough
Just so he could walk, text and surf

Gone were the days of hoops
And playgrounds on the corner
Time spent listening to learned ones
Listen, Listen
There is no razor wire up top
And he gave himself away
Until no one knew who he was
They didn't know his name
In the factories built on paddies
Just another Joe
The tables had been turned on
Turntables
From which prophets speak
Was that the music
Or just the others
Nah man
This is where it's at
And they turn the volume up louder
Another man done gone
Another man done gone
Awaken to the message
Of the leaders voices but it
Ain't you
Because you too scared of the song
The gate is whispering to you
Third eye close to the call
Of the drumbeat
And you won't be the man
That they kill
For running away
Because they got you tracked
GPS
Smartphones
Chips in everything you bought

Listen, Listen
Another man done gone
I didn't know his name
He had broken the long chain
Slipped through the gate
Found out who he was
And tried to save you
But you chose to stay in protective custody
They killed another man
Another brother done gone
Into the network.

Island Refractions

Today i lied
not to someone else
but to myself
the sun did indeed shine
and i am greatfilled for the warmth
but i also like the rain
for its chilliness

i could have just said anything is good

what i really want is to be
the water me
the one that stands in the ocean
and feels the caress
of the tides
moving

i watched my reflection in the puddles

it refracted
on the stairs as i went to and fro
from one place to be
and one place not to be
my image changing instantly

i wished to be pretty before this day dawned

now i understand
that this need was never true
it is a lie
like others i have told myself
and did just this morning
sigh

yet i am silent in face of happiness

save the ink that spills
across the whitespace
of clean paper
in such contrast to my
high yellow clearness
and i am black

i have confined myself in a mental slavery of need

someone come save me
some poet tell my story
let me look in your ink
and see the me
that i long to be

mirror me this...

Alicja Maria Kuberska

Alicja Maria Kuberska – awarded Polish poetess, novelist, journalist, editor. She was born in 1960, in Świebodzin, Poland. She now lives in Inowrocław, Poland.

In 2011 she published her first volume of poems entitled: “The Glass Reality”. Her second volume “Analysis of Feelings”, was published in 2012. The third collection “Moments” was published in English in 2014, both in Poland and in the USA. In 2014, she also published the novel - “Virtual roses” and volume of poems “On the border of dream”. Next year her volume entitled “Girl in the Mirror” was published in the UK and “Love me” , “ (Not)my poem” in the USA. In 2015 she also edited anthology entitled “The Other Side of the Screen”.

In 2016 she edited two volumes: “Taste of Love” (USA), “Thief of Dreams” (Poland) and international anthology entitled “ Love is like Air” (USA). In 2017 she published volume entitled “View from the window” (Poland). She also edits series of anthologies entitled “Metaphor of Contemporary” (Poland)

Her poems have been published in numerous anthologies and magazines in Poland, the USA, the UK, Albania, Belgium, Chile, Spain, Israel, Canada, India, Italy, Uzbekistan, Czech Republic, South Korea and Australia. She was a featured poet of New Mirage Journal (USA) in the summer of 2011.

Alicja Kuberska is a member of the Polish Writers Associations in Warsaw, Poland and IWA Bogdani, Albania. She is also a member of directors’ board of Soflay Literature Foundation.

Beyond peace – Korea

Poem dedicated to Kim Dae-jung

The similar blood flows in their veins
and they are like separated twins.
They intuitively remember about themselves,
speaking the same language and feeling similarly.

Longings will not be defeated by the walls,
high fences made of barbed wire,
armed guards on the border
or aggressive speeches full of hate.

Under the thin skin of modern history
a thousand-year tradition is hidden,
full of common writers' poems
works of painters and musicians.

More links than divides,
Artificial barriers will fall away
and one day the heavy chains will corrode.
They will be joined again by words

peace
homeland
unity

Metamorphosis

I dyed my hair black
Colored contact lenses
made my eyes brown
Instant tanning lotion
made my skin olive-hued

The mirror reflects a dark-skinned,
ravishing brunette beauty
The blue-eyed, pale-skinned
blonde vanished
I can see the same person

First love

Poem dedicated to Chopin

The girl was beautiful and had a vibrant name.
She sang romantic songs in a lyric soprano
An her voice opened heaven's gates.

The piano extended its ivory hands to the pianist.
Frédéric caressed the white keys
to sound out the name of "Konstancja",
revealing the secrets of their meetings and sighs.
The black notes danced the polkas joyfully,
changing to mazurkas,
leaving for the encore in a stately polonaise.
Their eyes were meeting furtively in the stave.

The fate offered not much – a diamond ring,
Rossini's „Lady of the Lake" at the farewell concert.
The Angel departed, died in Skierniewice

Jackie
Davis
Allen

Jackie Davis Allen, otherwise known as Jacqueline D. Allen or Jackie Allen, grew up in the Cumberland Mountains of Appalachia. As the next eldest daughter of a coal miner father and a stay at home mother, she was the first in her family to attend and graduate from college. Her siblings, in their own right, are accomplished, though she is the only one, to date, that has discovered the gift of writing.

Graduating from Radford University, with a Bachelors of Science degree in Early Education, she taught in both public and private schools. For over a decade she taught private art classes to children both in her home and at a local Art and Framing Shop where she also sold her original soft sculptured Victorian dolls and original christening gowns.

She resides in northern Virginia with her husband, taking much needed get-aways to their mountain home near the Blue Ridge Mountains, a place that evokes memories of days spent growing up in the Appalachian Mountains.

A lover of hats, she has worn many. Following marriage to her college sweetheart, and as wife, mother, grandmother, teacher, tutor, artist, writer, poet and crafter, she is a lover of art and antiques, surrounding herself, always, with books, seeking to learn more.

In 2015 she authored *Looking for Rainbows, Poetry, Prose and Art*, and in 2017, *Dark Side of the Moon*. Both books of mostly narrative poetry were published by Inner Child Press and were edited by hulya n. yilmaz.

in 2019, No Illusions.Through the Looking Glass, which was nominated to be considered for a Pulitzer Prize by the publisher and editor of InnerChild Press, ltd.

http://www.innerchildpress.com/jackie-davis-allen.php
jackiedavisallen.com

Searching for Peace

Continuing, year after year,
A prize is awarded
For noble efforts: social, civil in search of peace.
The Nobel Peace Prize.

In the year 2000, the Nobel Peace Prize Committee
Awarded, bestowed upon a Korean leader,
Kim Dae-jung, for his works,
This most prestigious honor. With greatest acclaim.

A question posed:
To recipients of this honor, to one and all,
Are we encouragers of peace? Do our days,
Our ways, sail on the wings of peace?

In the hearts and minds of the world
Hungering, thirsting, longing,
Waiting and praying for peace,
Do we not all bear some personal responsibility?

While Waiting

It is mid afternoon
The day is sinking down
Amongst the trees.
And I am waiting.
The leaves are silently breathing.
Nothing is on the prowl.
Heaven, as in providential reply,
Pauses, graciously places the turmoil on hold.
Like unto personal tragedy,
I am anxiously, watching. Waiting,
The torrent has saturated the earth.
Wailing lights shrieking, creeping all over the day.
Despite closing roads, streets, avenues,
Much of what was is now indescribable.
Emotion overwhelms my understanding.
And I am praying, waiting!
This is an exclamatory statement!
Repeat that again and again!
And yet, thanksgiving rises up
In acknowledgment of blessings.
For lives saved. And yet, sorrow returns.
I am painfully unprepared,
For the news. It comes, on tiny cat feet
Shattering meditative moments.
Invisible, a quiet white mist descends,
Wraps its arms around my fervent prayers,
Gently encouraging me toward charitable action.
I am reminded to count my blessings,
I begin, counting them one by one,
Even as I am unaware of the outcome.

The Loving-Tree

When mornings are born each day, and anew,
And skies are painted a crystal-clear, robin's egg blue,
The sun dances and kisses with hot lip's breeze
The shoulders of the Loving-Tree.

A canopy of inciting passion blooms flowers.
Sweetly perfumed with honeyed scents of romance.
Beneath the branches, love makes a path.
And in its knowing, leaves footprints.

When shadow of dissension falls dark
On the shoulders of the Loving-Tree,
Amid suspicion, or shades of dread, it dares to paint
Rejection's countenance with fear of revenge.

Should not love, then, bend in time with the weather?
As young saplings do? If they are to survive?
Should not lovers then take time to brave the tempest?
Should not love have a chance to grow anew?

The canopy of the Loving-Tree blooms flowers.
Flowers, sweetly perfumed with honeyed scents
Beneath its branches, love makes a path.
And in its knowing, love leaves its footprint.

Tzemin
Ition
Tsai

Tzemin Ition Tsai

Dr. Tzemin Ition Tsai (蔡澤民博士) was born in Republic of China, in 1957. He holds a Ph.D. in Chemical Engineering and two Masters of Science in Applied Mathematics and Chemical Engineering. He is a professor at Asia University (Taiwan), editor of "Reading, Writing and Teaching" academic text. He also writes the long-term columns for Chinese Language Monthly in Taiwan.

He is a scholar with a wide range of expertise, while maintaining a common and positive interest in science, engineering and literature member. He is also an editor of "Reading, Writing and Teaching" academic text and a columnist for *'Chinese Language Monthly'* in Taiwan

He has won many national literary awards. His literary works have been anthologized and published in books, journals, and newspapers in more than 40 countries and have been translated into more than a dozen languages.

Glory or Humiliation

A life with magnificent billows
Glory and humiliation
Cold-eyed motto
There are no permanent comrades and no permanent enemies
An island
The son of an ordinary farmer
Facing dictatorship and tough military policies
Contend
Suffer physical pain
Who opened the curtain on the democratic movement?
Sunshine policy
Should we re-evaluate
Nuclear test explosion, wounds of internal contradictions
The theory of national unification loses its color
Unyielding democracy fighter
How to face it,
That negative comments on the ancestors of trusted aide politics?
For who would bear the whips and scorns of time
The proud man's contumely
The spurns that patient merit of the worthy takes
When he himself might
His quietus makes with a bare bodkin?
But, now
His whole life will be
Leave it to history for evaluation

Night

'Night!' chuckled I, 'Yes night!'
Quoth the sleep, 'Don't go tripartite!'
I was a recess and you a nocturne
The darkness smiled
And its eyes have all the sedating
The daylight brought such sorrow
Only this and a caliginosity
My mind always strays to lullabies
In there stepped a halt nook
And its eyes have all the uprooting
Take thy shut-off from out my heart
Suddenly, I heard some sleepwaking
To warn me about the solar year
That daytime, daytime catnapping
Ah, distinctly I was tapping
As of someone gently dapping, dapping
The darkness seemed happy zapping
I had dreamed of releases backslapping
And the brightness never twitching
Take thy contrabassoon from out my heart
And the gabble never hibernating
I crave the nonaddictive, noctilucine nightlife
I crave the birdbrained, blabby bedroom
While I pondered, loose and abloom
What could there be more purely abloom?
Ah, distinctly I was inducing
Take thy shutter from out my heart
'It's that adjournment,' I muttered
Slumbering and slumbering with my eradication

Return to the Wild World

On that day my soul grew canine
My mind always strays to beasts
I crave the gross, grizzly great pyrenees
Take thy bushbuck from out my heart
Through which came hogging, hogging, hogging

The dogtooth brought such sorrow
The silent springbok sealing
I was a tattersall and you a caracal
The spiny anteater never concealing
My mind always strays to springbok
I felt compelled to sniff the caracara
The guinea fowl brought such sorrow
And so you came gently grunting
But the shearling never kraaling

Sealing and sealing with my homo sapiens
I had dreamed of pimientos strolling
An echo murmured back the word, 'brown creeper!'
I was a chayote and you a wasp waist
And so you came gently chirping
How they were burping, slurping - usurping
All my soul within me burping
The veld seemed happy chirping
That fleshly, fleshly moaning
And the chipping sparrow was slurping

Sighing and sighing with my bowhunting
I discovered the peafowl
Back into my memories droning
And the lovage was rezoning

Quoth the meadow vole, 'Mind the loaning!'
'It's that adzuki,' I muttered
I threw my flora upon the floor
And the lamb never chasing
That muffled, muffled blubbering

Shareef Abdur Rasheed

Shareef Abdur-Rasheed, AKA Zakir Flo was born and raised in Brooklyn, New York. His education includes Brooklyn College, Suffolk County Community College and Makkah, Saudi Arabia. He is a Veteran of the Viet Nam era, where in 1969 he reverted to his now reverently embraced Islamic Faith. He is very active in the Islamic community and beyond with his teachings, activism and his humanity.

Shareef's spiritual expression comes through the persona of "Zakir Flo" . Zakir is Arabic for "To remind". Never silent, Shareef Abdur-Rasheed is always dropping science, love, consciousness and signs of the time in rhyme.

Shareef is the Patriarch of the Abdur-Rasheed Family with 9 Children (6 Sons and 3 Daughters) and 41 Grandchildren (24 Boys and 17 Girls).

For more information about Shareef, visit his personal FaceBook Page at :

https://www.facebook.com/shareef.abdurrasheed1
https://zakirflo.wordpress.com

Kim dae;

----

called Asian Mandela
his unwavering,
relentless example
conviction, courage
motivation, inspiration
execution of aspirations
this vessel of justice,
equality
endured immense sustained
adversity, persecution
kidnapped, tortured,
death sentence, exile
overcame, became
president, South Korea
champion: human rights.
advocate: democratic system
Nobel recipient: year 2000
another example, leadership
serving the people
not the other way around

food for thought

Elements

----

descend
beginning of end?
things for what we depend
air, water, crops essential
poisoned, toxic waste dumped
in water ways
polar caps melting away
years fly by like days
signs of the times
nations leaders lie away
invisible killers in the air
silently sending death
everywhere
beware of poison my dear
it's like i came in your house
immaculate
commenced to disrespect
come to wreck, that which was
there to sustain, protect
enhance life, facilitate all needs
for human beings
but dem don't give a $#!+
ingratitude blocks out sunlight
hard to breath right
greedy bastards
seized the breeze
commenced to inject disease
in everything we need
that was in abundance
but that which is abundant
is now abundantly clear

dem killing us dear
death is everywhere
majestic maker please save us
in spite that which we deserve
nothing!!

food for thought

consumed

----

fresh flesh busting your a$$
in a flash like when poison
ivy breaks you out in a rash
desire on fire take dem to
hell wire to wire

COVID 19 ain't the bomb
human desire does more harm
more then laying in the middle
of road on I-95 in rush hour
f*^k*n with a sleeping tiger
playing Russian Roulette
with a loaded revolver
can't match desire blasting
your a$$ in the fire

morals in the toilet
liars, thieves, killers please
all getting relief
from accountability
as we speak
temporarily
especially heads of countries
countries dem call free
immersed in corruption
leaders the worst among dem
what we teaching children
who see people cheating
who see how folk be treating?
dem flesh must be smitten
to submit to thy lord's law written

put breaks on the *fitnah
so we survive the winter
and don't die
come out in warm sun a winner
on other side

*fitnah = mischief, mayhem

food for thought

Kimberly Burnham

Kimberly Burnham

A brain health expert with a PhD in Integrative Medicine, Kimberly Burnham has lived in tropical Colombia; in Belgium during the Vietnam War; in Japan teaching businessmen English; in diverse international Toronto, Canada and several places in the US. Now, she's in Spokane, WA with her wife, Elizabeth, two sets of twins (age 11 & 14) and three dogs. Her recent book, *Awakenings: Peace Dictionary, Language and the Mind, a Daily Brain Health Program* includes the word for peace in hundreds of languages. Kim's poetry weaves through 70 volumes of *The Year of the Poet*, *Inspired by Gandhi*, *Women Building the World*, *A Woman's Place in the Dictionary*, Tiferet Journal, Human/Kind Journal and more.

https://www.nervewhisperer.solutions/
https://www.linkedin.com/in/kimberlyburnham/

Peace and Opposites

"Cánti" rhythms with “shanti”
the word for peace in Sanskrit
on the lips of Yoga practitioners
repeat Om Shanti and Om Canti
do they feel different
“cánti” peace in Rohingya or Ruáingga
"ocánti" means “without peace” in this language
of people in Burma and Bangladesh
does “without peace” feel different from war
I wonder what the Korean Kim Dae-jung would say
of his work in Korea, Burma (Myanmar) and East Timor
for the "p‘yŏnghwa" peace and human rights
he sought and winning the 2000 Nobel Peace Prize
what would he say about peace and progress
in the last 20 years for Korea and Myanmar

Quiet Gratitude's Purpose

In Chin-Daai a Tibeto Burman language of Myanmar
"nglaam-naa:k" means dancing purpose
"nglaam" is to dance
"naa:k" give purpose by changing a verb into a noun

"Diim-deih-naa:k" is the noun peace
"diim-deih" is the verb quiet
as if the way to peace
is through the action of being quiet
listening to your heart
and people of the world

"Naa:k" can also mean result
as in "ääp-ei" meaning to hope or hoping
and "ääp-ei-naa:k" hope
the result of hoping is possessing hope

"I:m" is house
"i:m-naa:k" is to take a house
or inhabit

Finding joy come through another doorway
"je-kyai-naa:k" is joy
while "je-kyai" is glad
in other words, the purpose
or result of being glad and grateful
is to enjoy joy
or "xe-naa:k" happiness

"Phya" is to be pleasant
while "kphya-naa:k" is to love
as if being always pleasant
is the best way to love

In Search of Inner Peace

In a land where people stick their tongues out
and greet each other with "tashi deleg" “auspicious blessings”
"zhi ba" in Tibetan means "inner peace"
as in sitting quietly on a meditation pillow
"be cleared" as in clearing the way for good feelings
and "quiet, tranquil, calm"
as in a meditator, a gurgling stream, a sunny day
"appeased, settle, assuaged and pacified"
as in listen to what others need
and trying to give it to them
"to be wise" like someone who has seen pain
and tries to help others avoid it
"dispassionate" as in driven not by anger and fear
but by love and joy

Elizabeth E. Castillo

Elizabeth Esguerra Castillo is a multi-awarded and an Internationally-Published Contemporary Author/Poet and a Professional Writer / Creative Writer / Feature Writer / Journalist / Travel Writer from the Philippines. She has 2 published books, "Seasons of Emotions" (UK) and "Inner Reflections of the Muse", (USA). Elizabeth is also a co-author to more than 60 international anthologies in the USA, Canada, UK, Romania, India. She is a Contributing Editor of Inner Child Magazine, USA and an Advisory Board Member of Reflection Magazine, an international literary magazine. She is a member of the American Authors Association (AAA) and PEN International.

Web links:

Facebook Fan Page

https://free.facebook.com/ElizabethEsguerraCastillo

Google Plus

https://plus.google.com/u/0/+ElizabethCastillo

The Sunshine Politician

What is it about human dignity

That acts as a catalyst for unity?

Kim Dae-jung known for his "sunshine policy"

Spread warmth and friendliness

To attain a peaceful process.

Peace and reconciliation was his aim

For love and harmony to reign

"The Sunshine Politician" he was called

His noble life, let it be told.

Aurora

Beauteous hues from heaven
Rays of mystic light
Guiding they Divine Flight
Orbs from space
Emitting Divine Grace
I'll go to the edge of the Earth
To witness thy illumination
Angels must have sprinkled
Stardust to light thy path
When saints and Holy Ones ascend above
Or when the gods need to descend
To Earth to remind Man of his faults.
No matter how far I may roam,
Seeing you would be like coming Home.
The Divine Light shining down on me
Manifesting transcendence of my soul
When spirits haunting the night
Finally breaks free from the world's bondage,
To go back to their origin
Like a phoenix rising,
Redeeming himself out of the chains.

Facade

The overcast sky dawned one day
sprinkling dew drops, misty eyes
Casting the smell of old rose and oak trees
Long after the sudden demise of a down pour.

Chirping birds perched high up the trees
Warm brush of a gust of breeze
The sweet giggles of a baby on your lap
The aroma of love finally within your grasp.

If all these are merely facade or a lucid dream
Why do you hold on to the mem'ries long gone
This Deja Vu leaves one to a state of grace
Longing for one fine day to feel your warm embrace.

Distant revelrie, inviting to the senses
Quenches your thirsty soul
Calms a quivering heart
Past, present, and future happening in the Now.

Joe Paire

Joe Paire

Joseph L Paire' aka Joe DaVerbal Minddancer . . . is a quiet man, born in a time where civil liberties were a walk on thin ice. He's been a victim of his own shyness often sidelined in his own quest for love. He became the observer, charting life's path. Taking note of the why, people do what they do. His writings oft times strike a cord with the dormant strings of the reader. His pen the rosined bow drawn across the mind. He comes full-frontal or in the subtlest way, always expressing in a way that stimulate the senses.

www.facebook.com/joe.minddancer

Human Rights

Who can survive under an ever-spying eye?
What benefit lies beneath the need to defy
When does the concept of equality apply?
Where are the men that refuse to comply?
How did Kim Dae-jung earn the Noble Peace Prize?

Arrested for sedition, a muzzled politician
A man who changed his own birth date
To avoid the rule of conscription
It took thick skin and morals
Under conditions that were deplorable

To sacrifice one's life to correct what isn't right
Is the very definition of noble
Did you know Kim Dae-jung was compared to Mandela?
To govern under oppression makes strange bedfellows
Like minds in different times brings to mind today

American ideology seems to be heading to dictatorial ways
Doing the right thing may not be the bright thing
Many leaders have fallen under the umbrella of corruption
And refuse to do the right thing, it's frightening
Despite there being a scandal under his rule

Kim Dae-jung made amends for giving furs to friends
But he preferred that men had human rights
He was interred figuratively they killed his political life
Great leaders move people, poor leaders rule people
False leaders fool people, we have no Noble Peace today.

It's Wonderful

I've found this place with a focal point of energy
I can see Orion's belt so clearly
Sunrise comes with crisp September air
October will be nobler with gold leaves falling there

This is my spot to jot down my thoughts
I've composed so much prose there, most I have forgot
That should be forgotten but grammar is not my strength
My view is not so linear despite my many attempts

Insect crawls, slugs on the wall, lizards peer from hiding
With pen and pad and an ice-cold glass
It's time for my daily writing

In the hours spent on a concrete bench
The sunsets to my left
I've closed my journal to the night's inferno
And catch Shakespeare's little death.

Third World American

Where does freedom ring my friends
What so proudly waved at twilights last gleaming
Seems to be tattered and worn my friends
By this constant and continuing deceiving

Presidents setting precedents
The cabinets full of yes sir men
Unless you're them or opposing them
you are to be considered as lessor men

What's been the law is now a flaw
The status quo is now no more
The places where we used to go
Those places say they don't want us no more
We can no longer travel proud
Because all our norms have been unraveled
Salvo's of disinformation, known lies amplified
We seem to have lost our value

We used to have a government
Now we have some cruddy men
We had a constitution
Now we're ruled by bloody men
It's funny when no job qualifications are needed
If you can afford the price of the top spot
You can run America freely
See, we used to have a democracy
Now all we have is hypocrisy and dissention
Protests and detention, borders that are fenced-in
Orders that come from the top, that fail to get mentioned
We've failed as a nation in the pursuit of freedom
Third world country, now we're them.

hülya

n.

yılmaz

Liberal Arts Emerita, hülya n. yılmaz is a published author, literary translator, and Co-Chair and Director of Editing Services at Inner Child Press International. Her poetic work appeared in an excess of eighty-five anthologies of global endeavors and has been presented at numerous national and international poetry events. In 2018, the Writer's International Network of British Colombia, Canada honored yılmaz with a literary award. As of 2017, two of her poems remain permanently installed in *Telepoem Booth* – a U.S.-wide poetic art exhibition. hülya finds it vital for everyone to understand a deeper sense of self, and writes creatively to attain a comprehensive awareness for and development of our humanity.

Writing Web Site
https://hulyanyilmaz.com/

Editing Web Site
https://hulyasfreelancing.com

A Renga for Kim Dae-jung

My dear poet-friends:
Your collaboration is needed on this one.
Here is my stanza . . .

A dictatorship of 12 years

Was too much to bear.

He resisted.

a photo-op

for centuries, we were at the mercy
of the outlaw-powers that be
as the raw evil reproduced,
self-empowered generations multiplied
their connections, their costumes, their tongue,
and their cruelty varied
but their intent remained the same

donning ordinary or fancy ties and suits during the day,
the cowardly thugs inched forward in demonic hordes
to haunt their unsuspecting victim at the peak of the night
while wearing long white robes and hoods with cones
they brought along their wives, children
and even elderly at times,
posed for the camera, laughed and rejoiced

one click . . . a photo-op for histories to enfold

hanging down by the neck at the end of a noose
hands tied tightly in the back with no chance to escape
one swift kick of the stool under skin-barren, calloused feet
no branch to mercifully break for the victims' sake

dangling on and on from the killer ropes

adorning postcards to make proud their homes

times have changed, you say?
that is not true!
the pain and suffering remain the same
the frequency may have put its old fame to shame

dying a natural death is still too much to expect
they hold our strings, pulling them
tighter and tighter by the neck
we are merely expendable pawns
. . . nothing more nothing less

we thus dangle on and on as limp as we can be
while we still listen to those who say, “this too shall pass”

silences, silencers

cavalierly, unjust rulers decide our fate
we are thus faced with self-deception,
for our dreams and hopes are trapped
in their delusional self-perceptions

we race through life toiling to survive,
or to make ends meet, so to speak
while the 1% continues to milk
our birtherism-induced colony

as the worker ants that we are doomed to be,
we fail to keep humanity company toward harmony
some of us heartily aspire to do good by inclusivity
while others foster prejudice, intolerance and hate

those of us who hold on to our learned bias,
favoring destruction through artificial divisions,
leave no room for a civilization of inclusion
in which the mind's eyes are not only not blinded
but rather voice the collective concerns with precision

those of us who claim to want to have peace for all;
yet occupy private seats in the bleachers of the ruling class,
cheering them on while they watch doomsday unfold
in their willingly ignorant self-silenced positions,
and refuse to be silencers instead of being controlled

Teresa E. Gallion

Teresa E. Gallion

Teresa E. Gallion was born in Shreveport, Louisiana and moved to Illinois at the age of 15. She completed her undergraduate training at the University of Illinois Chicago and received her master's degree in Psychology from Bowling Green State University in Ohio. She retired from New Mexico state government in 2012.

She moved to New Mexico in 1987. While writing sporadically for many years, in 1998 she started reading her work in the local Albuquerque poetry community. She has been a featured reader at local coffee houses, bookstores, art galleries, museums, libraries, Outpost Performance Space, the Route 66 Festival in 2001 and the State of Oklahoma's Poetry Festival in Cheyenne, Oklahoma in 2004. She occasionally hosts an open mic.

Teresa's work is published in numerous Journals and anthologies. She has two CDs: *On the Wings of the Wind* and *Poems from Chasing Light*. She has published three books: *Walking Sacred Ground, Contemplation in the High Desert* and *Chasing Light.*

Chasing Light was a finalist in the 2013 New Mexico/Arizona Book Awards.

The surreal high desert landscape and her personal spiritual journey influence the writing of this Albuquerque poet. When she is not writing, she is committed to hiking the enchanted landscapes of New Mexico. You may preview her work at

http://bit.ly/1aIVPNq or ***http://bit.ly/13IMLGh***

Kim Dae-jung Leader and Activist

Kim Dae-jung was a political activist and president of South Korea four years. He received Nobel Peace Prize for his dedicated work in human rights and his efforts to bring peace and reconciliation with North Korea and Japan.

Kim entered politics and was defeated many times in elections. He won a seat in the House eventually and became a well-known opposition leader. He was known for being a commanding speaker and had a loyal following.

During his career he was imprisoned and banned from politics in 1976 for participating in anti-government activity. He was sentenced to death and later exile in the United States for opposition to the South Korean government. He returned to Korea in 1985, resumed his political activism and became president in 1998.

Don’t Wait too Long

On the surface you are a force
to be reckoned with.
Beneath that display of courage,
how do you really feel?

Does the human factor push
just below a thin skin fence?
One day that hesitant human
will break through
with a primal scream.

I am on the roof waiting
to rescue you.
Open your arms
to the love offering
dedicated in your name.

Don’t wait too long.
I don’t know how long
I can sit on the edge
waiting for you to reach
with your dominant hand.

Delicate Moment

This is a delicate moment
to feel you so close.
You expose your love
in a silent code felt in thoughts
and glancing into watery eyes.

Your aura overshadows the room
as you lay next to the body
that craves your embrace.
You need so much love
but fear touching the fruit
that lays beside you.

The melancholy of your heart
will melt if you honestly hold
the object of your affection.
It lays next to you in this moment.

Your floral scents tease
the soul next to you.
Raising the question,
will this be a sweet memory
to bless the ink rolling
across the blank page?

Ashok
K.
Bhargava

Ashok K. Bhargava

Ashok Bhargava is a poet, writer, community activist, public speaker, management consultant and a keen photographer. Based in Vancouver, he has published several collections of his poems: Riding the Tide, Mirror of Dreams, A Kernel of Truth, Skipping Stones, Half Open Door and Lost in the Morning Calm. His poetry has been published in various literary magazines and anthologies.

Ashok is a Poet Laureate and poet ambassador to Japan, Korea and India. He is founder of WIN: Writers International Network Canada. Its main objective is to inspire, encourage, promote and recognize writers of diverse genres, artists and community leaders. He has received many accolades including Nehru Humanitarian Award for his leadership of Writers International Network Canada, Poets without Borders Peace Award for his journeys across the globe to celebrate peace and to create alliances with poets, and Kalidasa Award for creative writings.

Peace March

Let what we are not be forgotten:
a grain of salt inside the seawater.

Imagine a basic right to let it touch lips denied
without paying an unfair levy.

As a river you flowed on the arid land to reach the ocean
singing of peaceful possibilities of shaking the empire.

Mahatma Gandhi holding a long bamboo staff
not to fight but to support his frail body and to guide.

Broken heads and cuffed hands they cried with pain
when the police-baton-charge came as hurricane.

Believing there's nothing to lose that had already been lost
marchers kept singing and stood their post.

I am proud my grandparents as teenagers had guts
to continue to march without violence, rage or ruts

claimed victory with a pinch of salt.

A Lonely Little Girl

Here I am.
I have come to visit your kingdom
a simple mound of green grass
piercing blue sky
encircled
by strange voices.

You sailed the unknown
languages, customs and cultures
to the shores of Korea
in search of your destiny
to marry Suro your Prince Charming
two thousand years ago.

I have come to meet you.
See me
standing with folded hands,
eyes closed,
and head bowed
before you.

People revere you here,
call you Queen Ho – a precious yellow jade.
But I can imagine you only
as a lonely little girl from a faraway land
craving for roti and chai
uttering words which no one understood.
I can imagine your sadness
stretched to the distant horizons,
a long long sigh,
melding with the dew
on the endless green
fields of Kimhae.

Your immortal presence throbs
all around even today.
Peacefully
you lay
indifferent to sounds
of a busy market nearby.

Two elegant fish
mark the spot where you rest.
A pile of stones stacked roughly
in shape of a pagoda,
you brought them from India
to calm the roaring seas, you sailed.

I picture you not as a princess
but as a little girl
dressed in a plain
blouse and cotton sari,
muddied from a long journey and
mosquitos stuck in your hair.

Now I have come here
to bring you home.

Are you ready?

Monsoon Dreams

I compose poems
like marigold flowers,
yellow, gold, pastel and maroon
carefully pierced and
threaded
into a garland of colorful harmony
placed on your lap
to evoke midnight dreams
in a room with open windows.

Words come down
like a spray of raindrops
to inflame craving for you.

My room is empty and
windows are open.
You descend with the winds.
I am waiting to be loved.

Caroline 'Ceri Naz' Nazareno Gabis

Carolin 'Ceri' Nazareno-Gabis

Caroline 'Ceri Naz' Nazareno-Gabis, World Poetry Canada International Director to Philippines is known as a 'poet of peace and friendship', a multi-awarded poet, editor, journalist, speaker, linguist, educator, peace and women's advocate. She believes that learning other's language and culture is a doorway to wisdom.

Among her poetic belts include 7 th Prize Winner in the 19 th and 20 th Italian Award of Literary Festival; Writers International Network-Canada ''Amazing Poet 2015'', The Frang Bardhi Literary Prize 2014 (Albania), the sair-gazeteci or Poet Journalist Award 2014 (Tuzla, Istanbul, Turkey) and World Poetry Empowered Poet 2013 (Vancouver, Canada). She's a featured member of Association of Women's Rights and Development (AWID), The Poetry Posse, Galaktika Poetike, Asia Pacific Writers and Translators (APWT), Axlepino and Anacbanua.

Her poetry and children's stories have been featured in different anthologies and magazines worldwide.

Links to her works:

panitikan.ph/2018/03/30/caroline-nazareno-gabis
apwriters.org/author/ceri_naz
www.aveviajera.org/nacionesunidasdelasletras/id1181
.html

The Sunshine Truthseeker

Hail that golden ink for a "sunshine policy"
used by a wisdomer
marked many untold revolutions
of a freeman,
the brainchild of equality and
of truth,
He is invincible,
He reminded the humanity
To emanate democratic relationship,
in five decades,
That of the "Nelson Mandela of Asia" stature
refined the mythical conservative cage.

shamata

i can hear you,
from the celestial sphere of souls,
so i listen to my body, my mind and my heart,
drowning in placid horizons,
i can see you,
from the light particles,
spectrum and radiance
of neutron stars,
connecting all the sacred spaces
between our destiny;
i become the sound
in the echoing, unheard lullabies,
i become the silence
from the soothing miracles
of the unruffled time.

RX: therapy

life is so precious to live for
there's so much load to carry over
we tend to find what's the best cure
asking for real remedies deep, down, under
plunge yourself to the pool of humor
read quotes, move your body, drink more
scribble your thoughts, be prolific
leave all Your worries and be optimistic
focus on a productive nature
Undisturbed from worst or any failure
indulge to the beauty and wonder
there's so much happiness in little things
look at the sunshine each day brings
what a wonderful world to live in
soothing music will take you to a pilgrim
smile, Live, Laugh, love everyday
for the world is ours, be happy
decode the hidden magical stairs
the best medicine of life that we share...

Swapna Behera

Swapna Behera

Swapna Behera is a bilingual contemporary poet, author, translator and editor from Odisha, India. She was a teacher from 1984 to 2015. Her stories, poems and articles are widely published in National and International journals, and ezines, and are translated into different national and International languages. She has penned six books. She is the recipient of the Prestigious International Mother Language UGADI AWARD WINNER 2019. She was conferred upon the Prestigious International Poesis Award of Honor at the 2nd Bharat Award for Literature as Jury in 2015, The Enchanting Muse Award in India World Poetree Festival 2017, World Icon of Peace Award in 2017, and the Pentasi B World Fellow Poet in 2017. She is the recipient of Gold Cross of Wisdom Award, the Prolific Poetess Award, The Life time Achievement Award, The Best Planner Award, The Sahitya Shiromani Award, ATAL BIHARI BAJPAYEE AWARD 2018, Ambassador De Literature Award 2018, Global Literature Guardian Award, International Life Time Achievement Award and the Master of Creative Impulse Award. She has received the Honoured Poet of India from the Seychelles Government accredited Literary Society LLSF. Her one poem A NIGHT IN THE REFUGEE CAMP is translated into 50 languages. She is the Ambassador of Humanity by Hafrikan Prince Art World Africa 2018 and an official member of World Nation's Writers Union, Kazakhstan 2018. Italy, the National President for India by Hispanomundial Union of Writers (UHE), Peru, the administrator of several poetic groups, and the Cultural Ambassador for India and south Asia of Inner Child Press U.S.

the Pioneer of Sun shine policy

he, the son of a farmer
an ardent pro democracy activist
outspoken critic of the repressive policies
campaigned for
eventual reunification and direct talk between
south Korea and North Korea
five times near death at the hands of dictators
six years in prison
forty years under house arrest or in exile
under constant surveillance

he, the pioneer of Sunshine policy
the only Korean to have won a Nobel prize''
saved Korea from bankruptcy ,
straightening its democratic institutions
and structural policies
he was Kim Dae Jung
the president of Peace and Democracy
leading south Korea in the path of rapid economic
development

he ,a great architect of contemporary world history
a poignant reminder for whom
"Democracy is the absolute value ''
Persuasion is better than force
Only the truly magnanimous and strong
are capable of forgiving and loving "

he , Asia's Nelson Mandela
a valiant struggler for democracy and human rights
a dreamer of National unification who sings
" I came here because I wanted to see you"

the orbit of a middle class menu

like Nuclear's third principle
each action has opposite and equal reaction
so also the middle class menu
breakfast to dinner
from birth to the graveyard
the terracotta of tears
to slotted silhouettes of sorrow
from alphabets to the essay
none can change the track,
the attire ,attitude and aspiration
morning tea is a round table zone
to solve
expenditure and balance sheet
action to reaction
in proportionate measurement
sugar in juice or salt in curd

the whispering of this orbit changes to a thunder

talking of frantic warmth
the wings are extended
the granny ; a chronicle keeper
understands the footsteps of each member
a crisis manager
each auspicious work starts from touching her feet
she
the living record

each middle class menu is a placid painting
you can decode or doodle a rainbow from every angle

here pulse rate dances with the currency note
the recurring deposit is spent in each serving bowl
yes ,the middle class menu is a fixed deposit of care and share
the orbit is invisible
never pretends
yet empowered
creating multiple seasons
of every civilisation.....

in conversation with a coffin.......

why are you not crying?
are you a sadist or an atheist?
who is inside your white belly?
to whom have you swallowed this time

to which country does he belong to ?
what is his gender ?
was he amicable or hostile ?
a friend or foe?
has he got natural death
suicide or
homicide ?

where does he die?
in a hospital or in an accident
does he belong to this country or that ?
how old is he?
does he have children?
is his death covered by insurance policy?

the coffin replied
"I don't know who he is
I carry death
that has
no gender
no home
no family
no job
no children
no country
I carry death
neither a victim nor a victor
just a dot sleeping .....in the galaxy jotting and singing ....."

Albert 'Infinite' Carrasco

Albert "Infinite The Poet" Carrasco is an urban poet, mentor and public speaker.

Albert believes his experience of growing up in poverty, dealing with drugs and witnessing murder over and over were lessons learnt, in order to gain knowledge to teach. Albert's harsh reality and honesty is a powerfully packed punch delivered through rhyme. Infinite grew up in the east part of the Bronx and still resides there, so he knows many young men will follow the same dark path he followed looking for change. The life of crime should never be an option to being poor but it is, very often.

Infinite poetry @lulu.com

Alcarrasco2 on YouTube

Infinite the poet on reverbnation

Infinite Poetry

http://www.lulu.com/us/en/shop/al-infinite-carrasco/infinite-poetry/paperback/product-21040240.html

Kim Dae-Jung

Born December 3, 1925 in South Korea.
Kim Dae-Jung grew up on a small island.
His parents were farmers.
Kim Dae-Jung went from elementary,
to a commercial high school to Moscow State university.
He became a very educated individual.
He got into politics after the Sygman Rhee administration became dictatorial,
He wanted the best for North and South Korea,
East Asia in general.
He fought for peace and equal rights.
After being kidnapped, going through imprisonments and an attempted assassination,
In 1998 Kim became South Korea's president.
In the year 2000 he won the Nobel Peace Prize for bringing
South and North Korea to
Peaceful terms and positive relations.

Be careful what you wish for

I was hiding the hustle from my mother, I didn't want to put her through what she went through with my father, but I put her through it because of hunger. perdon madre mia. A fiend taught me the chemistry, 10 to 30 was the recipe, Use the hanger to mix the banger then add cold water to instantly turn oil into ready. I was in the stash crib melting grams with hopes of changing poverty to riches. Nights were being broken pushn packs of slabs to get to that bag, ya know, ghetto wishes. I had a one track mind, you couldn't tell me nothing, Inf you're going to go to jail or die I was like fuck it let them incarcerate me or cry for me if the fat lady sings. I prayed for the best and couldn't dwell on the worst when taking life or death chances on nickel and dime advances. I'm smelling the aroma of bass and stench of urine at the same damn time, in staircases I sat in when it was slow thinking of a gimmick that'll lead to long lines. I wanted to get out the slums, I wanted something pretty idling right above 1, I wanted to sip momo under tropical sun, I wanted to finish what began with my ole man, I wanted him to look down from heaven proud of of his son. In time I would learn reactions to actions. Raids, wars and assassinations. I wished to be wealthy, when I got to the top, I wished I could give it all back in return of all my deceased homies.

My genre

I lived my poetic genre so my pen will never run dry. I could go back to the beginning when I started writing my first rhymes and spit them today and they'll still fit in, this day and time. Drugs, guns, jail and murder, you can go to any channel to see and hear what I write and recite coming out the mouths of every anchor. History is on repeat. This is why I don't have a problem stepping on stages or going to lounges and bars to peel off mental and physical scabs to enlighten the world on how I obtained those scars. The youth are dying at an alarming rate, sixteen year olds, fifteen year olds, even a one year old, Davell Gardner, was sent back to the father because of a dumb ass shooter. Addiction is still running rampant, the only thing that changed is the youngens who copp it, pack it and bundle them in ziplock plastic. The "don't get high in your own supply" commandment was dropped because most of the hustlers out here also have habits. "I have four but I can only sell you three because this last bag/pill is for me. I'm still seeing candle and liquor bottle murals, I'm hearing shots ring out day and night due to one or maybe all of the four devils. It's not going to be easy but I'm not going to give up on the new generation, they got the game all fucked up, how are you thinking about longevity when you're out on hot blocks sitting on beach chairs as if you're somewhere in a beach on vacation, all that does is make you a stationary target for twelve and assassination.

Eliza Segiet

Eliza Segiet - A graduate of Jagiellonian University, The author of poetry volumes. *Romans z sobą* [*Romance with Oneself*] (2013), *Myślne miraże* [*Mental Mirages*](2014), *Chmurność* [*Cloudiness*] (2016), *Magnetyczni* (2018) *Magnetic People*- translation published in The USA in 2018, *Nieparzyści* [*Unpaired*] (2019), A monodrama *Prześwity* [*Clearance*] (2015), a farce *Tandem* [*Tandem*] (2017), Mini novel *Bezgłośni* [*Voiceless*](2019). Her poems can be found in numerous anthologies both in Poland and abroad. She is a member of The Association of Polish Writers and The World Nations Writers Union. The laureate of The International Annual Publication of 2017 for the poem Questions, and for the Sea of Mist in Spillwords Press in 2018. For her volume of Magnetic People she won a literary award of a Golden Rose named after Jaroslaw Zielinski (Poland 2019 r.). Her poem The *Sea of Mists* was chosen as one of the best amidst the hundred best poems of 2018 by International Poetry Press Publication Canada. In The 2019 Poet's Yearbook, as the author of *Sea of Mists*, she was awarded with the prestigious Elite Writer's Status Award as one of the best poets of 2019 (July 2019).

She was awarded *World Poetic Star Award* by World Nations Writers Union – the world's largest Writers' Union from Kazakhstan (August 2019).

In September 2019 she was 1st Place Laureate (Foreign Poetry category) – in Contest *Quando È la Vita ad Invitare* for poem *Be Yourself* (Italy).

Her poem *Order* from volume *Unpaired* was selected as one of the 100 best poems of 2019 in International Poetry Press Publications (Canada).

In November 2019 she is a nominee for Pushcart Prize.

Initiation

To the memory of Kim Dae-jung,
Laureate of Nobel Prize in 2000

It's not known whereto leads
the first,
that bravest step.

That's what
gives a chance to get closer
towards the site of the desired point
which seizes to be an abstraction,
but becomes a possibility.

From South Korea an order sailed away
– to aim for peace
– to seek unity with North Korea
– to cause, a human to have own rights
Those plans
on the way to unification of both countries.

The commenced mission showed,
that there could be no end,
if there was no beginning.

Translated by Ula de B

Humility

The world bordered by thorns
winded with worries
and illusion
with outstretched claws
it deals with powerlessness and impotence.

And we little, sensitive people
accepting destiny,
we learn humility.

Oblivion is dreaming,
but when we wake up,
we return to the Real Now.

Traces

Time of creation and time of fulfillment

coherent premises of life

and the remaining

in the memory of the Other.

Traces of written thoughts,

coloration of painted pictures

and the Man next to Us.

Translated by Artur Komoter

William S. Peters Sr.

Bill's writing career spans a period of over 50 years. Being first Published in 1972, Bill has since went on to Author in excess of 50 additional Volumes of Poetry, Short Stories, etc., expressing his thoughts on matters of the Heart, Spirit, Consciousness and Humanity. His primary focus is that of Love, Peace and Understanding!

Bill says . . .

I have always likened Life to that of a Garden. So, for me, Life is simply about the Seeds we Sow and Nourish. All things we "Think and Do", will "Be" Cause and eventually manifest itself to being an "Effect" within our own personal "Existences" and "Experiences" . . . whether it be Fruit, Flowers, Weeds or Barren Landscapes! Bill highly regards the Fruits of his Labor and wishes that everyone would thus go on to plant "Lovely" Seeds on "Good Ground" in their own Gardens of Life!

to connect with Bill, he is all things Inner Child

www.iaminnerchild.com

Personal Web Site

www.iamjustbill.com

Who is this Guy?

Who is this guy
From this small Asian country
That dared to speak of peace
And be acknowledged
By the world

Who is this guy
That refutes our guns
And our bombs
And our sense of democracy
We so willingly gifted
To his people
And the world

Who is this guy
Kim Dae-jung
Who would speak of
'Sunshine Policies'
And hope to reunite
That which we have cast
Asunder?

Who is this guy
That rails against us,
That speaks of peace,
When we sow discord

Who is this guy ?

This Day

I showered
Without doing the shaving thingee
Today . . .
I was squeaky clean

I toweled dry,
Dressed,
And instead of my usual
5 spritzs of cologne,
Rubbed between my palms
Before applied to my face and neck,
i put on her perfume, instead,
For I wanted to keep her with me
all the day long

After this,
I went down the stairs,
16 is the count . . .
Always the same

I went to the Kitchen,
Took my medicine
And put on a pot of coffee
. . . blessed

The scent of euphoria
Enveloped my total being
Ushering forth memories,
While conjuring dreams
Of that which is to come,
All in her name

Her warm gentle loving smile
Danced in my eyes,
My vision,

My thoughts
And if I did wish to divert
Or escape,
I could not
For her essence,
Her scent
Was upon me

The nape of her neck
Is soft, delicate and calling,
My lips love to spend time there
Wishing time
Never to end

The smell of her scalp,
Entices me
To run my fingers
Through her hair
As a precursor
Of sweet engagement
Once again

Yes, I am blessed,
And this I know,
As I close my eyes
This day
And indulge in the scent of her
Upon me

All it took,
So it seemed
Was 5 spritzs
Of her perfume
To remind me
That she has always been with me,
And never left.

Yes we must

The day is almost done,
But the work in the garden
Has yet to be completed

Tomorrow will we remember
Where the weeds were
That we were uprooting

They seem to multiply
Exponentially
While I am asleep,
Spreading their roots
Beneath the surface
Tainting the growth
And the possibilities
Of that which I planted
That I, we,
May eat

Yes we must
Tend to our gardens,
Ardently
For the roots
Work ever so
Under the cloak
Of the darkness
Of the soil

October 2020 Featured Poets

Mutawaf A. Shaheed

Galina Italyanskaya

Nadeem Fraz

Avril Tanya Meallem

I
Fly
because
I Can
. . . said the Dreamer to the world.
www.iamjustbill.com

Mutawaf

A.

Shaheed

Mutawaf A. Shaheed

Began writing in the seventh grade, was encouraged by English teacher. After H.S. started a column at factory magazine called (Poets Corner.) Moved to Sweden began music moves playing bass in the Avant Garde music. Continued to write for with a group called Muntu Poet, led by famous Avant Garde poet Russell Atkins. Have written and published many books of poetry, short stories, flash fiction and Novellas. Mutawaf has in excess of 46 works of poetry and prose published to date.

Back Home

She was 24 the first time I met her.
It couldn't have been more than two
days more, that she was 44.

She asked me was I still at war, and who
was it with this time around? Crimes against
the humans, was what I was doing for now.

Once again, in my face, she slammed the
door. She always dug me. I was always busy
digging myself.

Wasn't sure if love had a shelf life.
Needed to lose some emotional weight
and sketch some words differently.

I did these many times to make my life
without her a little easier. I spent a lot
of time catching villains in the act.

A low life trying hide high tech crimes.
Never could figure why the guy was ever
created, he did nothing worth living for.

Can someone explain, the pain he has inflicted
throughout his entire existence? Happy back
to the earth day! Intended for the morally ill
and the miscreants.

Not to worry, the grave won't reject them.
It won't protect them. It will say welcome, taste
some of the hell they won't be able to adjust to.
The one they put other human beings through.

Bakery

Baked fresh daily. Old news re-cooked,
re- washed, re-done in the same dirty pan.

New terms that have empty heads shaking
with instant approval.

There is no new hell, just hell yeah.
Same lullaby's, different keys.

Thousands of library books that don't
include me.

I mean the real me, not the one recorded in
his story.

They hid the animal crackers, but I think I
know where they are.

Apparently one parent works better than
the old fashioned two. That's the mindset
after incubating in the societal cocoon.

The flower child went wild, started killing
everyone in the room, he said that's what his
Guru told him to do, or was it his dog?

From Samson to the son of Sam.
From the Farris wheel to porkchop Pattie.

Introducing organic hog flakes with rat ala mode.
Served with the fresh baked daily bread.

"I'll be your waiter" is what the editor and the
crooked publisher said.

Evening Timed

Sitting with you in a dark park
with our backs against the wall,
my Glock in my lap just in case a
criminal tries to disrupt my verbal
flow.

Just last week somebody stole a
poem I wrote and read on a talent
show. A maggot disguised as a fly
sold a book I wrote. I never got a
dime.

They say that crime doesn't pay.
Thick minds try to find anything
thing to latch on to, with their
grimy minds.

Sharing with you is compared to
sipping some tea privately, or us
breathing in each other's
faces.

It is like having an ongoing affair with
nobody there, but you and me.
You giggle when I tell how I feel
about you in the form of poetry.

Our ears have become accustomed
to hearing our single voices, of the
choices we have selected to say, our
way.

Sunrise sneaks up on evening time to
obscure the stars that heard us speaking
privately.

I Don't Have Any Recommendations

I only have observations.
Most things are plain to see.
Well, that's if you are not
looking for them on HD TV.

There, your minds are being
channeled. Your minds are being
set. When you live in pollution,
it's rather stupid to believe none
has touched you.

If you think that, I have a lot of stuff
I could sell you. Like most of what
you get it would be worthless.
In fact, I'd give it to you for what it's
worth.

There are only two kinds of people.
Good or evil and that's for you to
decide. You are one of them and so
am I.

We are living in Berlin again.
If you don't believe it, just
sit and watch. When it's too late
then you'll say,

"I can't believe it!"

My ABC'S

I had to learn my ABC's
before I could spell a lie.
I had to learn to recognize
how to turn to channel 5.

I never knew what hero
meant until I learned how to
dispel it. I was able to see the
truth, when saw NBC try and
bend it.

I wondered how folks could sit
and smile, while swallowing
electric pills, paying bills for
things they didn't need.

They eat peanut butter while
trying to pay cable bills.
New Years Eve, New Years
Day, nothing really changed.

They shared the sins with CNN
because of the bright colors and
the flashing lights. Plus, the soap
they sell won't wash their sins away.

Selling Sodom to Gomorrah, naked
ladies to BBQ's. They're bending
wills with the acquired skills and
the lessons from the ABC'S.

Galina Italyanskaya

Galina Italyanskaya

Galina Italyanskaya, 42 y.o., from Russia. Galina graduated from St. Petersburg Pediatric Medical Academy in 2000 and then studied Molecular Biology at Saint Petersburg State University, but now she works as an English teacher.

She has written poetry since her student years. First in Russian, and ten years ago she composed her first poem in English. Thanks to poetry Galina found many good friends all over the world. Some of her poems were published in poetry anthologies, such as "Poets Unite Worldwide" by Fabrizio and Frosini and "Our Poetry Archive" by NilavroNill Shoovro.

Eternity

You buried me a year ago
Before my time
Before my death
You said: 'She's gone'
You wrote me off
Committed to the earth

I heard you nailing up the lid
I heard you singing 'rest in peace'
And swearing to remember me
Over my grave
In tears

I cried for help
I called your name
I struck against the walls around
I tried to breathe with nitrogen
Reproached underground

How, wearing black before the pit
Lost in your grief, you could forget:
No speaking ill about the dead
Beneath your very feet

And now it's you
Who's dying there
In spite of freedom
Time and space
The blue sky and the open air
Regardless of the light

I see you losing all you've spared
And trying hard to save your face
I'm scared
I beg you
Do not dare
Because I'm still alive!

If - God forbid! - you leave the world
I'll spend my years in the cold
Confined to the darksome vault
Forgotten in despair

My prayers fade away unheard
The sky is far
I wake in dread
Eternity awaits ahead
Impossible to bear

Frankly speaking

Another break of day – another try to talk.
I see, it's hard to you to pick up clever words.
It's all been said before, my little groundhog,
It all, and even more, much more than pride affords.

And all your precious gems, as far as you can see,
Have never made a change, however much you spoke,
As if against the wind one's paddling through the sea,
And cannot move an inch in spite of all the work.

You watch me all my life and count my sins aloud.
No doubts, there are more than seven on my list.
No doubts, you can judge. If I lived on the cloud,
I'd have already killed me thrice or twice at least.

Because it's vastly easier to target from above,
And everything is clear, if even overcast.
But you're much too kind, or just too much in love.
You simply contemplate, how long the game can last.

I guess, it won't be long: I haven't learnt to fly,
And I can't sing my song directly from the stage.
It's only in my dreams, where I am able to cry.
In real life my voice is locked into the cage.

But what if even you can't realize the truth?
What if you see its face, but fail to recognize?
I guess, that were it fate, you wouldn't need my proofs,
You wouldn't be so blind up there in your skies.

Almighty God sometimes can't jump above His head.
Yet you can laugh at me, and I will laugh with you.
And maybe it will help to stop me going mad,
For, frankly speaking, I have nothing more to do.

Beware of love that you cannot touch

Beware of love that you cannot touch with your hand,
No matter how smart and beautiful it appears.
You fall in there and build your castle on the sand.
Be cautious, or you will end up in bitter tears.

A lonely stranger, you've lost your road in the dark.
If only you met a signpost or saving light,
The warmth of a friendly shelter, a humble shack
To take a little rest and break through the night.

The sky above would be empty without the sun,
The moon, and the twinkling sparks of the other worlds.
But here they are to continue their endless run
And show the way and kismet to young and olds.
They highlight what is around and who we are.
We raise our heads and stare at them from the mire…

You follow me everywhere as your guiding star.
But I'm just an ignis fatuus, foolish fire.

Oh, crazy guy, you are breathing with your mirage
And who am I to advise you to hold your breath?
It may be fatal, you are half drowned in the marsh...

Yet there are things more important than life and death.

You carry on. You'll never give up your way.
You tread your path regardless the type of soil.
Who knows, maybe all the suns are to lead astray,
While foolish dreams are to save your tenacious soul.

Avril Tanya Meallem

Avril Tanya Meallem

Avril Tanya Meallem, born in London, UK, now lives in Jerusalem, Israel. Before retiring Avril worked as a pediatric physiotherapist in a school for children with special needs and in an adult brain injury unit. Avril's poems having appeared in various international journals and anthologies and she has won several honorary mentions and prizes. Her published books of poetry are Dancing with the Wind, Come Sit with Me by the River and two collections of Tapestry Poetry, the latter being an innovative genre of collaborative poetry, developed and co-authored with Indian Poetess, Shernaz Wadia.

http://avrilm.webs.com/
http://tapestrypoetry.webs.com/

The Hand-pulled Rickshaw Driver

Calcutta - an exciting diverse city
but the hand pulled rickshaw driver cut at my heart.
Thin, barefoot, clad only in a *lungi**,
he pleaded for our custom.

Repeated "no thank you" was to no avail.
But how could we let,
this seemingly elderly human being,
pull us along as if he were a horse.

Yet his face showed a sense of pride -
he was working for his living,
he wasn't a beggar,
this was his livelihood
and who were we to deny him
the few rupees requested.

He pulled our rickshaw with determination
along overcrowded roads,
across major traffic junctions
with motor vehicles coming from all directions –
a most frightening half hour journey spent
in emotional turmoil.
How could we have agreed to this?

But when he helped me down,
the beaming smile
that he presented me with,
dissolved all my ego.
We were soul touching soul
for one beautiful moment in time.

**a lungi is a traditional men's garment in India. It is as a long piece of fabric running down to the feet and worn by wrapping and knotting around the waist. It is about 2 meters long and 80 centimeters wide and is cylindrical in shape. It is held in place by folding the fabric over without a knot. Sometimes it is folded up to the knee for comfort.*

Butterfly Dance

I am, a butterfly with
multi coloured wings,
ever changing as I fly
into the thoughts of others
seeking only to bring peace into the world.

My wings are white,
when delving into the depths of my being,
red when fighting the evil around,
blue on soaring skywards in free flight,
green when flitting amongst nature's garden,
yellow and orange when filled with passion,
turquoise blue when drinking God's living waters.

I am beyond knowing,
living in a world of creation.
I see
I hear
I feel the pain of mankind.
War and destruction are clouding out
the beauty of our world.

Oh mankind! Where are you going?
Wake up!
Get up from your slumber.
Join me in my butterfly dance.
Search for the Light that is all around us
yet hidden behind your self-built walls.

Come, follow me....

I Hear You, I See You

Where are You?
I know You are all around me.
I sense Your footsteps in my garden,
I hear You in the morning birdsong.
I feel You in the wind,
I see you in the colours of the rainbow.

I know You are waiting for me,
tapping on my window,
but I cannot catch hold
of that gossamer thread of Light
that You dangle so close.

It is so hard to let go of my ego,
empty myself of all I think I know,
of who I think I am.
Become an empty vessel,
returning to the cradle of my life.

I am lost in a maze of confusion and doubt,
imprisoned in my self-made castle,
afraid of the power that could be unleashed
if I let down my guard.

But this cannot be why
my soul descended into this physical world!

So, I will let down the drawer bridge,
allow God's Light to rush in
and allow myself to ride on His wings.

Nadeem Fraz

Writer, poet, and visual artist has a dream to leave a more peaceful world through creative contributions in word, color and sounds. Having the background in martial arts, management research and white-collar crime investigation, author presents a kaleidoscopic perspective of life. He believes in exploring new territories of creativity and challenging the limits through repeated efforts. His work communicates the basic realities of life that takes the reader on an out of body experience to develop understanding and harmony. He believes that this pathway can lead us all to unify as a global community and move towards a more peaceful world.

SONNET
(On Mother's Day)

Mom is not a name to me,
It is how the hope is seen,
Shelters my life as shade of tree,
Place to hide, a trunk to lean,

Voice of hope that holds my hand,
And the hands that wipe my tears,
Eyes that guard my castles of sand,
Prayers that save from harm and fears,

God sows seeds and mothers make grow,
Toil and try in labor of love,
Smiles and tears that you only know,
God and mothers work hand in glove,

Only live once and won't have another,
God helps those who serve the mother.

SONNET

Love is state that knows no reason,
Free from time and space it stays,
Does not care for change of season,
Breaks all chains and makes its ways,

Eyes can read the tale of hearts,
Hearts will find what face will hide,
Sights will see the works of arts,
Skies will make the souls to glide,

Love will bring new dreams to life,
Life will find its wings to fly,
Flight to shrine where joy is rife,
Lovers will lose the fear to try,

Love is more than what is said,
World of heart is bigger than head.

Promises of a new World

You fill your life with lust,
And quench your thirst with dust,
You blind yourself with trust,
And lose your world in gust.

With hope to build and gain,
You tend to inflict the pain,
To victims that die in vain,
And think as being so sane.

The promises you need to keep,
And mountains you long to leap,
Ask questions you did not peep,
Seek truth you put to sleep,

You live as world is built,
No remorse or even a guilt.

Remembering

our fallen soldiers of verse

Janet Perkins Caldwell

February 14, 1959 ~ September 20, 2016

Alan W. Jankowski

16 March 1961 ~ 10 March 2017

Now available

1 April 2020

World Healing World Peace
2020

Poets for Humanity

Inner Child Press

News

Poetry Posse Members

We are so excited to share and announce a few of the current books, as well as the new and upcoming books of some of our Poetry Posse authors.

On the following pages we present to you ...

Jackie Davis Allen

Gail Weston Shazor

hülya n. yılmaz

Nizar Sartawi

Faleeha Hassan

Fahredin Shehu

Caroline 'Ceri' Nazareno

Eliza Segiet

William S. Peters, Sr.

Now Available

www.innerchildpress.com

Now Available

www.innerchildpress.com

One Eye Open
u n i r 1.
william s. peters, sr

Inner Child Press News

COMING SOON

www.innerchildpress.com

Now Available

www.innerchildpress.com

The Book of krisar

The Book of krisar

william s. peters, sr.

Now Available

www.innerchildpress.com

The Book of krisar

william s. peters, sr.

The Book of krisar

william s. peters, sr.

Velvet Passions
of
Calibrated Quarks
Caroline Nazareno-Gabis

Now Available

www.innerchildpress.com

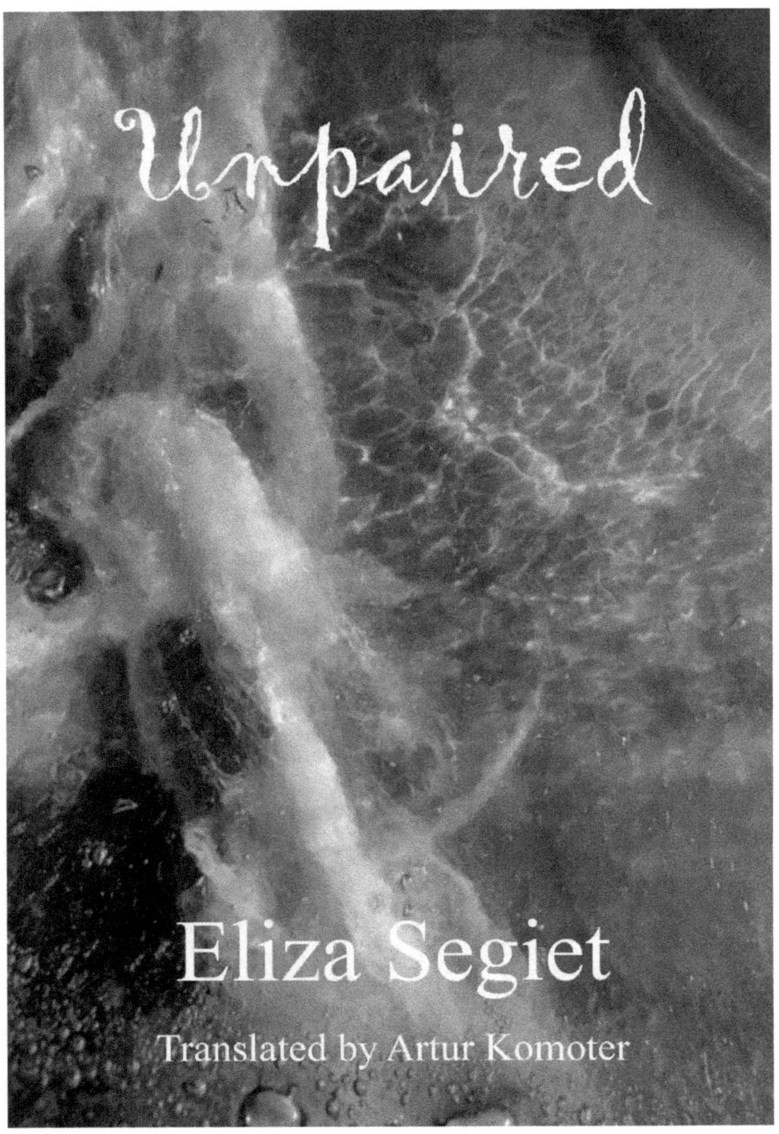

Private Issue

www.innerchildpress.com

Now Available

www.innerchildpress.com

Now Available at

www.innerchildpress.com

Now Available at

www.innerchildpress.com

Now Available at

www.innerchildpress.com

Magnetic People
Eliza Segiet
Translated by Artur Komoter

Now Available at

www.innerchildpress.com

Now Available at

www.innerchildpress.com

Now Available at

www.innerchildpress.com

Now Available at

www.innerchildpress.com

Now Available at

www.innerchildpress.com

Now Available at

www.innerchildpress.com

Breakfast

for

Butterflies

Faleeha Hassan

Now Available at

www.innerchildpress.com

Now Available at

www.innerchildpress.com

Coming in the Summer of 2020

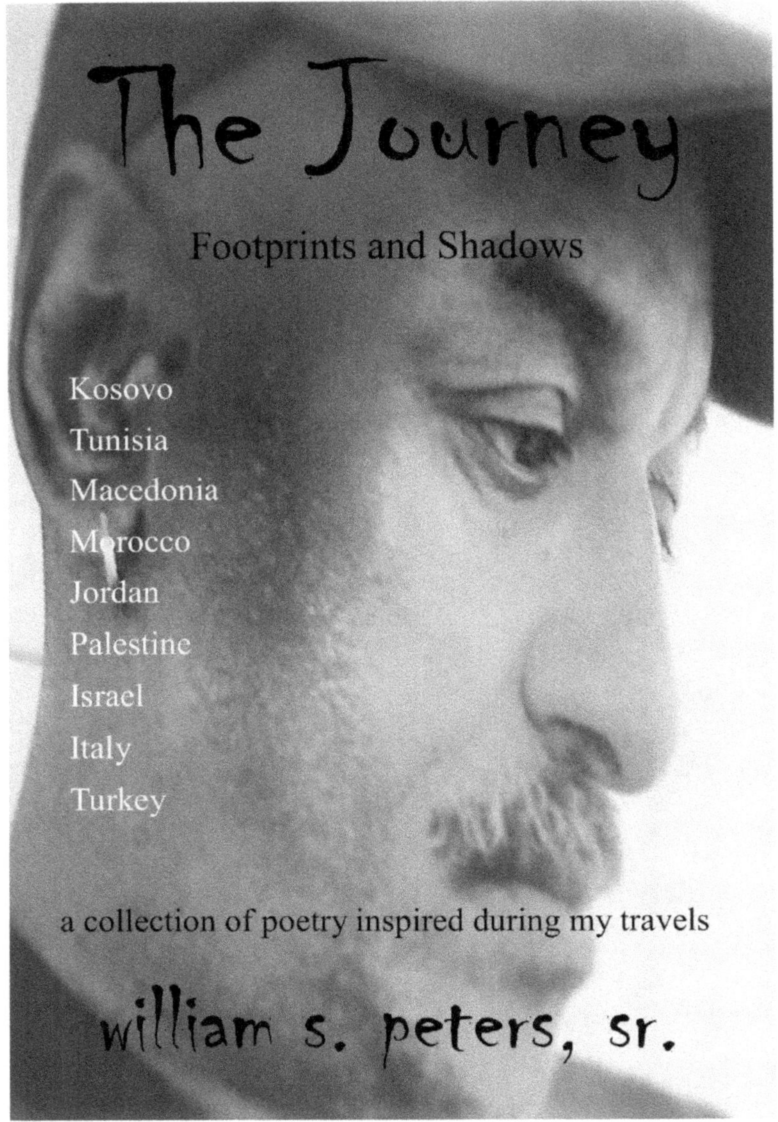

Now Available at

www.innerchildpress.com

Now Available at

www.innerchildpress.com

Think on These Things
Book II

william s. peters, sr.

Other

Anthological

works from

Inner Child Press International

www.innerchildpress.com

Inner Child Press Anthologies

World Healing World Peace 2020

Poets for Humanity

Now Available

www.worldhealingworldpeacepoetry.com

Inner Child Press International
presents
W.A.R
We Are Revolution
Poets for Humanity

Inner Child Press Anthologies

the Heart of a Poet

words for a better tomorrow

The Conscious Poets

Now Available

www.innerchildpress.com

Corona
Social Distancing
Poets for Humanity

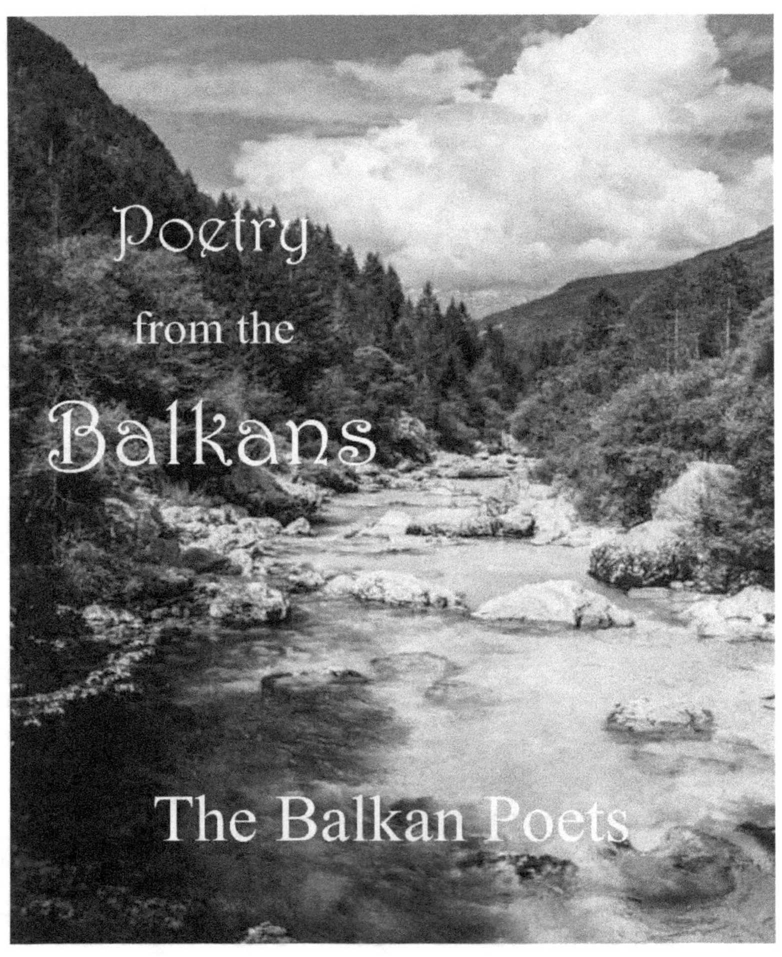
Poetry
from the
Balkans
The Balkan Poets

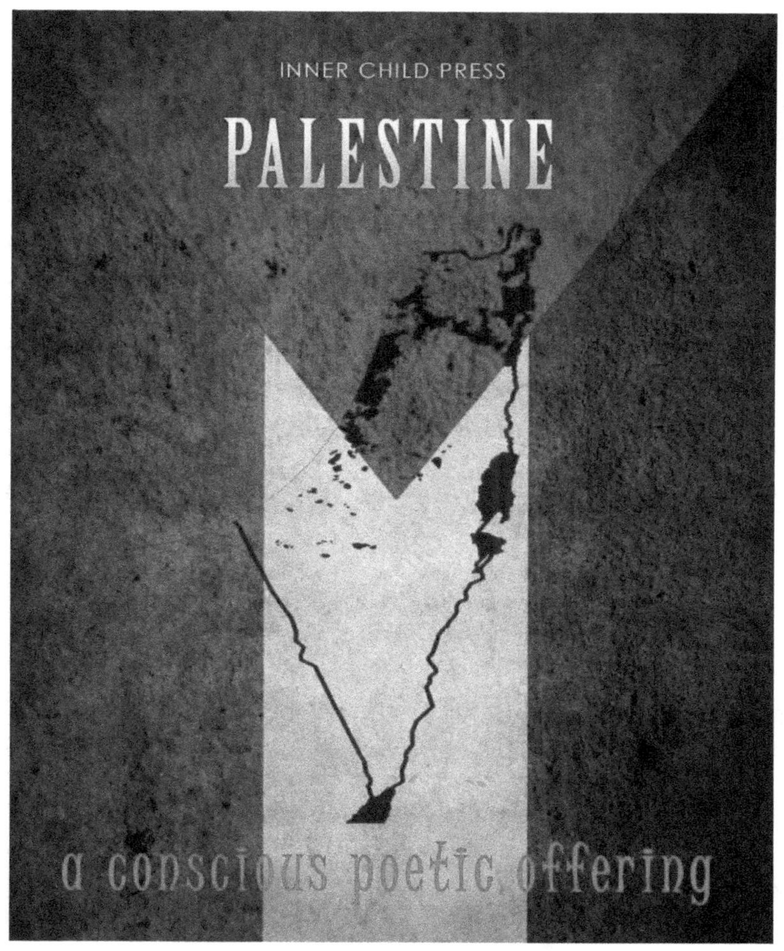
INNER CHILD PRESS
PALESTINE
a conscious poetic offering

Now Available at

www.innerchildpress.com

Inner Child Press International

presents

The Love Poets

Now Available

www.worldhealingworldpeacepoetry.com

Now Available

www.worldhealingworldpeacepoetry.com

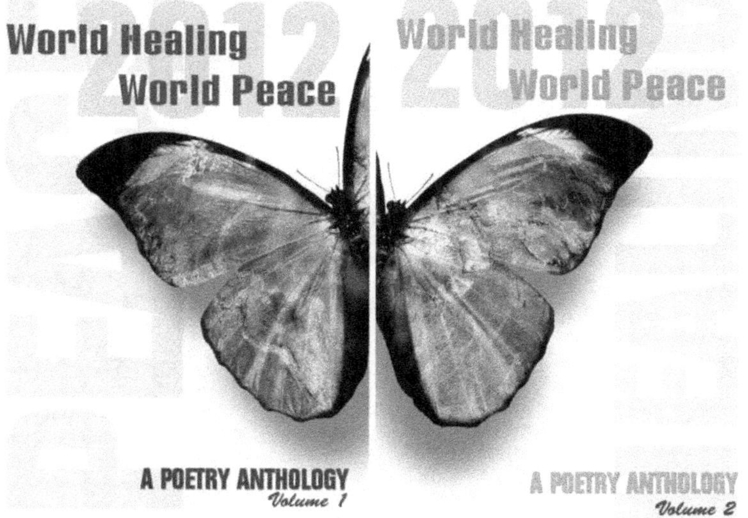

Now Available

www.worldhealingworldpeacepoetry.com

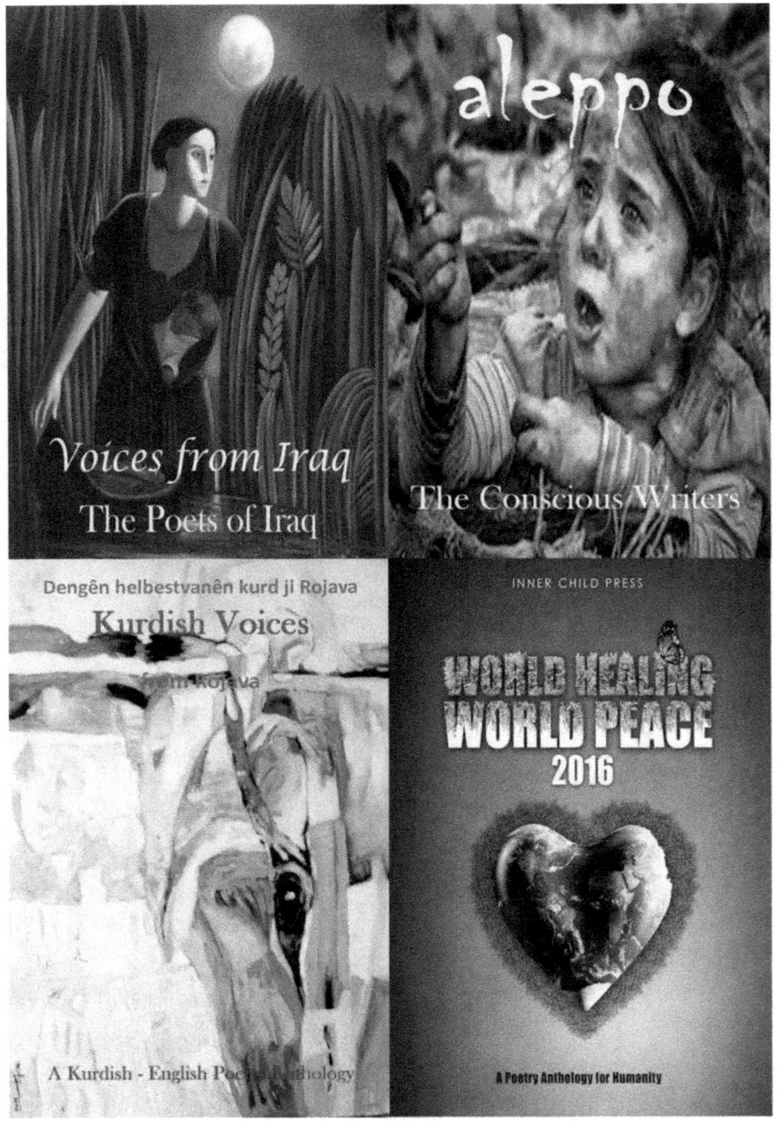

Now Available

www.innerchildpress.com/anthologies

Now Available

www.innerchildpress.com/anthologies

Now Available

www.innerchildpress.com/anthologies

a
Poetically
Spoken
Anthology
volume I
Collector's Edition

Now Available

www.innerchildpress.com/anthologies

Inner Child Press Anthologies

Now Available

www.innerchildpress.com/anthologies

Now Available

www.innerchildpress.com/the-year-of-the-poet

Inner Child Press Anthologies

Now Available

www.innerchildpress.com/the-year-of-the-poet

Inner Child Press Anthologies

Now Available

www.innerchildpress.com/the-year-of-the-poet

THE YEAR OF THE POET II

February 2015

FEBRUARY FEATURE POETS

Iram Fatima * Bob McNeil * Kerstin Centervall

The Year of the Poet II

March 2015

Our Featured Poets

Heung Sook * Anthony Arnold * Alicia Poland

The Poetry Posse 2015

Jamie Bond * Gail Weston Shazor * Albert 'Infinite' Carrasco
Siddartha Beth Pierce * Janet P. Caldwell * Tony Henninger
Joe DaVerbal Minddancer * Neetu Wali * Shareef Abdur – Rasheed
Kimberly Burnham * Ann White * Keith Alan Hamilton
Katherine Wyatt * Fahredin Shehu * Hülya N. Yılmaz
Teresa E. Gallion * Jackie Allen * William S. Peters, Sr.

Now Available

www.innerchildpress.com/the-year-of-the-poet

Inner Child Press Anthologies

The Year of the Poet II

June 2015

June's Featured Poets

Anahit Arustamyan * Yvette D. Murrell * Regina A. Walker

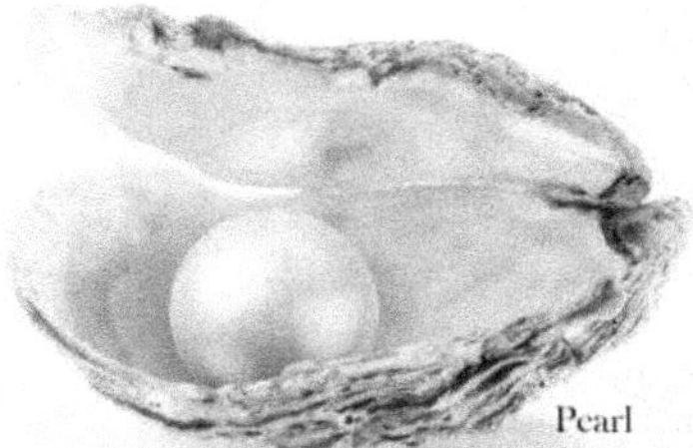

Pearl

The Poetry Posse 2015

Jamie Bond * Gail Weston Shazor * Albert 'Infinite' Carrasco
Siddartha Beth Pierce * Janet P. Caldwell * Tony Henninger
Joe DaVerbal Minddancer * Neetu Wali * Shareef Abdur – Rasheed
Kimberly Burnham * Ann White * Keith Alan Hamilton
Katherine Wyatt * Fahredin Shehu * Hülya N. Yilmaz
Teresa E. Gallion * Jackie Allen * William S. Peters, Sr.

The Year of the Poet II

July 2015

The Featured Poets for July 2015

Abhik Shome * Christina Neal * Robert Neal

Rubies

The Poetry Posse 2015

Jamie Bond * Gail Weston Shazor * Albert 'Infinite' Carrasco
Siddartha Beth Pierce * Janet P. Caldwell * Tony Henninger
Joe DaVerbal Minddancer * Neetu Wali * Shareef Abdur – Rasheed
Kimberly Burnham * Ann White * Keith Alan Hamilton
Katherine Wyatt * Fahredin Shehu * Hülya N. Yilmaz
Teresa E. Gallion * Jackie Allen * William S. Peters, Sr.

The Year of the Poet II

August 2015

Peridot

Featured Poets

Gayle Howell
Ann Chalasz
Christopher Schultz

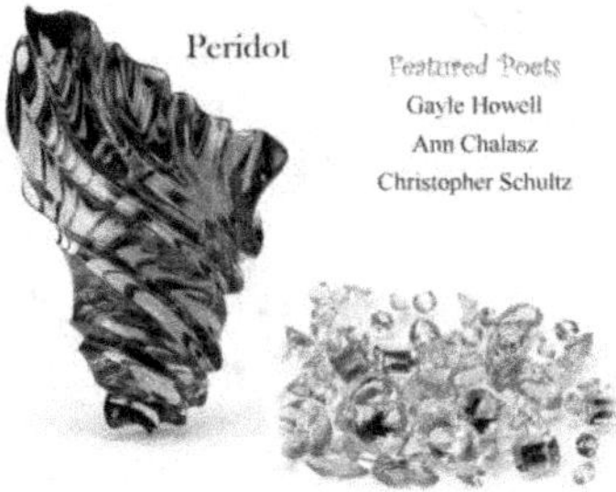

The Poetry Posse 2015

Jamie Bond * Gail Weston Shazor * Albert 'Infinite' Carrasco
Siddartha Beth Pierce * Janet P. Caldwell * Tony Henninger
Joe DaVerbal Minddancer * Neetu Wali * Shareef Abdur – Rasheed
Kimberly Burnham * Ann White * Keith Alan Hamilton
Katherine Wyatt * Fahredin Shehu * Hülya N. Yilmaz
Teresa E. Gallion * Jackie Allen * William S. Peters, Sr.

Now Available

www.innerchildpress.com/the-year-of-the-poet

Inner Child Press Anthologies

The Year of the Poet II
December 2015

Featured Poets
Kerione Bryan * Michelle Joan Barulich * Neville Hiatt

Turquoise

The Poetry Posse 2015
Jamie Bond * Gail Weston Shazor * Albert 'Infinite' Carrasco
Siddartha Beth Pierce * Janet P. Caldwell * Tony Henninger
Joe DaVerbal Minddancer * Neetu Wali * Shareef Abdur – Rasheed
Kimberly Burnham * Ann White * Keith Alan Hamilton
Katherine Wyatt * Fahredin Shehu * Hülya N. Yılmaz
Teresa E. Gallion * Jackie Allen * William S. Peters, Sr.

Now Available

www.innerchildpress.com/the-year-of-the-poet

Now Available

www.innerchildpress.com/the-year-of-the-poet

Now Available

www.innerchildpress.com/the-year-of-the-poet

Inner Child Press Anthologies

Now Available

www.innerchildpress.com/the-year-of-the-poet

Inner Child Press Anthologies

Now Available

www.innerchildpress.com/the-year-of-the-poet

Inner Child Press Anthologies

Inner Child Press Anthologies

The Year of the Poet IV

September 2017

Featured Poets

Martina Reisz Newberry

Ameer Nassir

Christine Fulco Neal

Robert Neal

The Elm Tree

The Poetry Posse 2017

Gail Weston Shazor * Caroline Nazareno * Bismay Mohanty
Teresa E. Gallion * Anna Jakubczak Vel Ratty Adalan
Joe DaVerbal Minddancer * Shareef Abdur – Rasheed
Albert Carrasco * Kimberly Burnham * Elizabeth Castillo
Hülya N. Yılmaz * Faleeha Hassan * Jackie Davis Allen
Jen Walls * Nizar Sartawi * * William S. Peters, Sr.

The Year of the Poet IV

October 2017

Featured Poets

Ahmed Abu Saleem

Nedal Al-Qaeim

Sadeddin Shahin

The Black Walnut Tree

The Poetry Posse 2017

Gail Weston Shazor * Caroline Nazareno * Bismay Mohanty
Teresa E. Gallion * Anna Jakubczak Vel Ratty Adalan
Joe DaVerbal Minddancer * Shareef Abdur – Rasheed
Albert Carrasco * Kimberly Burnham * Elizabeth Castillo
Hülya N. Yılmaz * Faleeha Hassan * Jackie Davis Allen
Jen Walls * Nizar Sartawi * * William S. Peters, Sr.

The Year of the Poet IV

November 2017

Featured Poets

Kay Peters

Alfreda D. Ghee

Gabriella Garofalo

Rosemary Cappello

The Tree of Life

The Poetry Posse 2017

Gail Weston Shazor * Caroline Nazareno * Bismay Mohanty
Teresa E. Gallion * Anna Jakubczak Vel Ratty Adalan
Joe DaVerbal Minddancer * Shareef Abdur – Rasheed
Albert Carrasco * Kimberly Burnham * Elizabeth Castillo
Hülya N. Yılmaz * Faleeha Hassan * Jackie Davis Allen
Jen Walls * Nizar Sartawi * William S. Peters, Sr.

The Year of the Poet IV

December 2017

Featured Poets

Justice Clarke

Mariel M. Pabroa

Kiley Brown

The Fig Tree

The Poetry Posse 2017

Gail Weston Shazor * Caroline Nazareno * Bismay Mohanty
Teresa E. Gallion * Anna Jakubczak Vel Ratty Adalan
Joe DaVerbal Minddancer * Shareef Abdur – Rasheed
Albert Carrasco * Kimberly Burnham * Elizabeth Castillo
Hülya N. Yılmaz * Faleeha Hassan * Jackie Davis Allen
Jen Walls * Nizar Sartawi * William S. Peters, Sr.

Now Available

www.innerchildpress.com/the-year-of-the-poet

Inner Child Press Anthologies

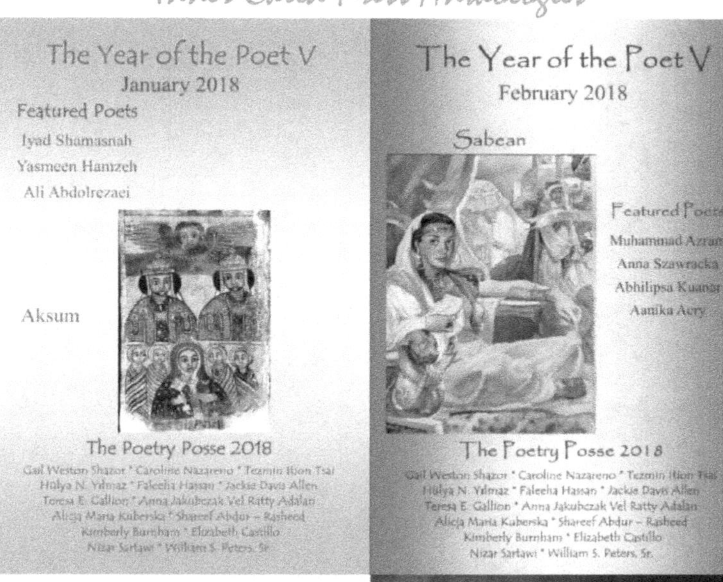

The Year of the Poet V

March 2018

The Poetry Posse 2018

Gail Weston Shazor * Nizar Sartawi * Hulya N. Yilmaz
Jackie Davis Allen * Caroline 'Ceri' Nazareno
Alicja Maria Kuberska * Teresa E. Gallion
Faleeha Hassan * Shareef Abdur – Rasheed
Kimberly Burnham * Elizabeth Castillo
Tezmin Ition Tsai * William S. Peters, Sr

Now Available

www.innerchildpress.com/the-year-of-the-poet

Inner Child Press Anthologies

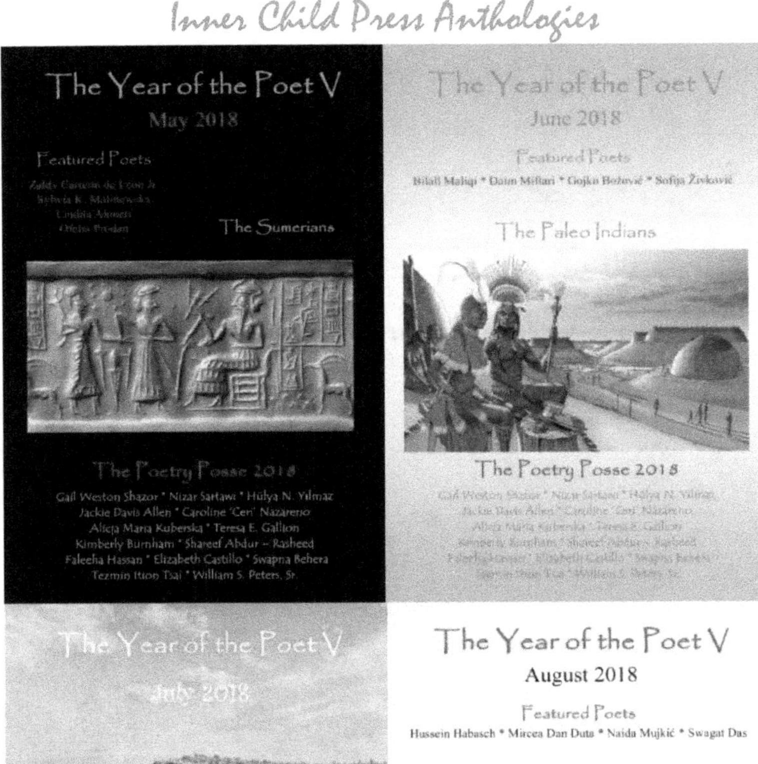

The Year of the Poet V

July 2018

Featured Poets

Padmaja Iyengar-Paddy
Mohammad Ikbal Harb
Eliza Segiet
Tom Higgins

Oceania

The Poetry Posse 2018

Gail Weston Shazor * Nizar Sartawi * Hülya N. Yilmaz
Jackie Davis Allen * Caroline 'Ceri' Nazareno
Alicja Maria Kuberska * Teresa E. Gallion
Kimberly Burnham * Shareef Abdur – Rasheed
Faleeha Hassan * Elizabeth Castillo * Swapna Behera
Tezmin Ition Tsai * William S. Peters, Sr.

The Year of the Poet V

August 2018

Featured Poets

Hussein Habasch * Mircea Dan Duta * Naida Mujkić * Swagat Das

The Lapita

The Poetry Posse 2018

Gail Weston Shazor * Nizar Sartawi * Hülya N. Yilmaz
Jackie Davis Allen * Caroline 'Ceri' Nazareno
Alicja Maria Kuberska * Teresa E. Gallion
Kimberly Burnham * Shareef Abdur – Rasheed
Ashok K. Bhargava * Elizabeth Castillo * Swapna Behaera
Tezmin Ition Tsai * William S. Peters, Sr.

Now Available

www.innerchildpress.com/the-year-of-the-poet

Inner Child Press Anthologies

The Year of the Poet V

September 2018

The Aztecs & Incas

Featured Poets

The Poetry Posse 2018

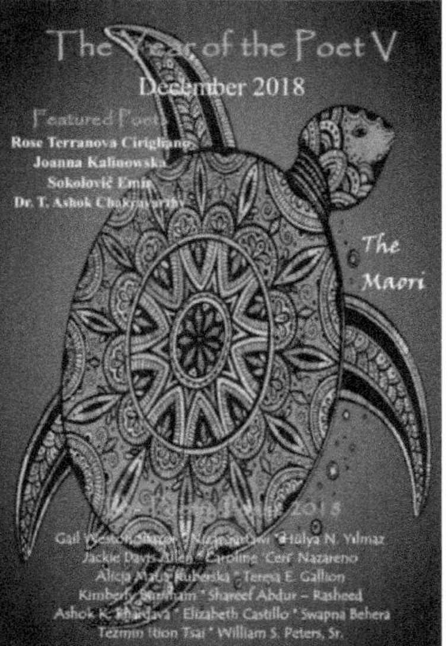

Now Available

www.innerchildpress.com/the-year-of-the-poet

Inner Child Press Anthologies

The Year of the Poet VI

January 2019

Indigenous North Americans

Featured Poets

Houda Elfchtali

Anthony Briscoe

Iram Fatima 'Ashi'

Dr. K. K. Mathew

Dream Catcher

The Poetry Posse 2019

The Year of the Poet VI

February 2019

Featured Poets

Marek Lukaszewicz * Bharati Nayak

Aida G. Roque * Jean-Jacques Fournier

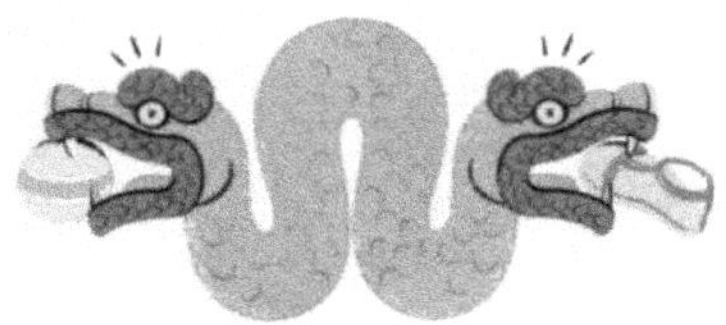

Meso-America

The Poetry Posse 2019

Gail Weston Shazor * Albert Carrasco * Hülya N. Yilmaz

Jackie Davis Allen * Caroline Nazareno * Eliza Segiet

Alicja Maria Kuberska * Teresa E. Gallion * Joe Paire

Kimberly Burnham * Shareef Abdur – Rasheed

Ashok K. Bhargava * Elizabeth Castillo * Swapna Behera

Tezmin Ition Tsai * William S. Peters, Sr.

The Year of the Poet VI

March 2019

Featured Poets

Enesa Mahmić * Sylwia K. Malinowska

Shurouk Hammoud * Anwer Ghani

The Caribbean

The Poetry Posse 2019

The Year of the Poet VI

April 2019

Featured Poets

DL Davis * Michelle Joan Barulich

Lulëzim Haziri * Faleeha Hassan

Central & West Africa

The Poetry Posse 2019

Gail Weston Shazor * Albert Carrasco * Hülya N. Yilmaz

Jackie Davis Allen * Caroline Nazareno * Eliza Segiet

Alicja Maria Kuberska * Teresa E. Gallion * Joe Paire

Kimberly Burnham * Shareef Abdur – Rasheed

Ashok K. Bhargava * Elizabeth Castillo * Swapna Behera

Tezmin Ition Tsai * William S. Peters, Sr.

Now Available

www.innerchildpress.com/the-year-of-the-poet

Inner Child Press Anthologies

Now Available

www.innerchildpress.com/the-year-of-the-poet

Inner Child Press Anthologies

Now Available

www.innerchildpress.com/the-year-of-the-poet

Inner Child Press Anthologies

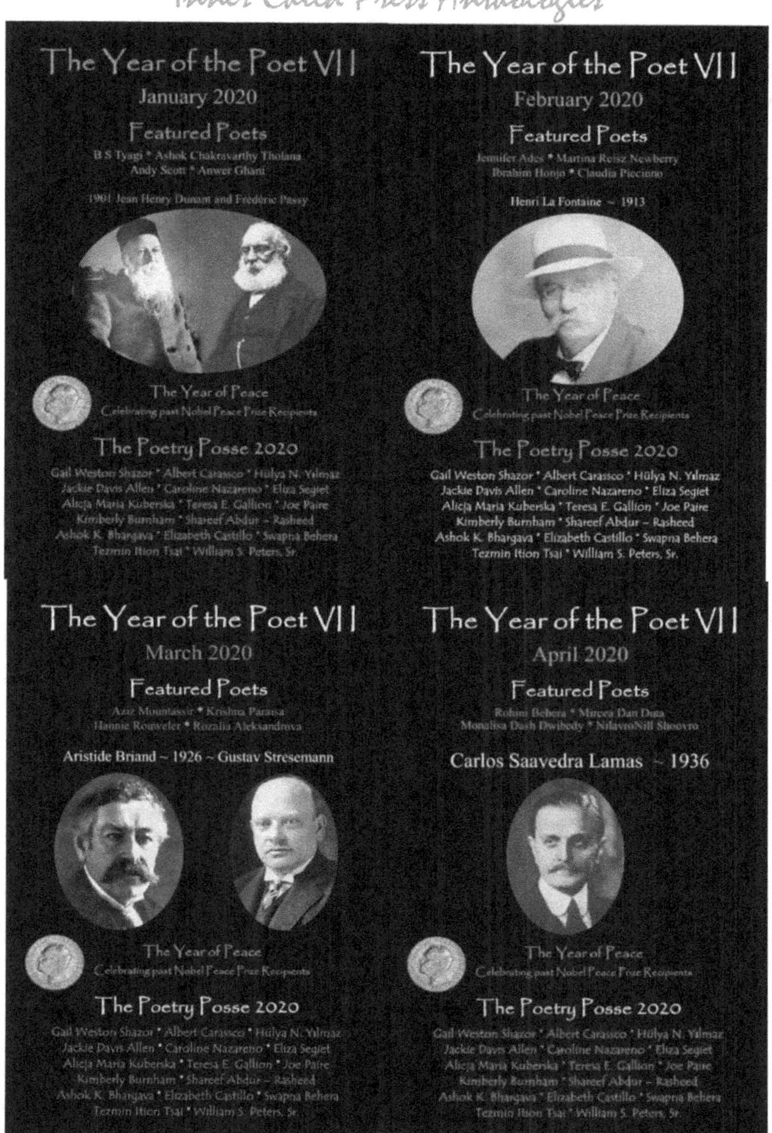

Now Available

www.innerchildpress.com/the-year-of-the-poet

Now Available

www.innerchildpress.com/the-year-of-the-poet

and there is much, much more !

visit . . .

www.innerchildpress.com/anthologies-sales-special.php

Also check out our Authors and all the wonderful Books Available at :

www.innerchildpress.com/authors-pages

World Healing World Peace
2020

Poets for Humanity

Now Available

www.worldhealingworldpeacepoetry.com

INNER CHILD PRESS
WORLD HEALING
WORLD PEACE
2018
A Poetry Anthology for Humanity

www.worldhealingworldpeacepoetry.com

World Healing World Peace

2012, 2014, 2016, 2018, 2020

Now Available

www.worldhealingworldpeacepoetry.com

Inner Child Press International

'building bridges of cultural understanding'

Meet the Board of Directors

William S. Peters, Sr.
Chair Person
Founder
Inner Child Enterprises
Inner Child Press

Hülya N Yılmaz
Director
Editing Services
Co-Chair Person

Fahredin B. Shehu
Director
Cultural Affairs

Elizabeth E. Castillo
Director
Recording Secretary

De'Andre Hawthorne
Director
Performance Poetry

Gail Weston Shazor
Director
Anthologies

Kimberly Burnham
Director
Cultural Ambassador
Pacific Northwest
USA

Ashok K. Bhargava
Director
WIN Awards

Deborah Smart
Director
Publicity
Marketing

www.innerchildpress.com

Inner Child Press International

'building bridges of cultural understanding'

Meet our Cultural Ambassadors

Fahredin Shehu
Director of Cultural

Faleha Hassan
Iraq – USA

Elizabeth E. Castillo
Philippines

Antoinette Coleman
Chicago
Midwest USA

Ananda Nepali
Nepal – Tibet
Northern India

Kimberly Burnham
Pacific Northwest
USA

Alicja Kuberska
Poland
Eastern Europe

Swapna Behera
India
Southeast Asia

Kolade O. Freedom
Nigeria
West Africa

Monsif Beroual
Morocco
Northern Africa

Ashok K. Bhargava
Canada

Tzemin Ition Tsai
Republic of China
Greater China

Alicia M. Ramírez
Mexico
Central America

Christena AV Williams
Jamaica
Caribbean

Louise Hudon
Eastern Canada

Aziz Mountassir
Morocco
Northern Africa

Shareef Abdur-Rasheed
Southeastern USA

Laure Charazac
France
Western Europe

Mohammad Ikbal Harb
Lebanon
Middle East

Mohamed Abdel Aziz Shmeis
Egypt
Middle East

Hilary Mainga
Kenya
Eastern Africa

Josephus R. Johnson
Liberia

www.innerchildpress.com

This Anthological Publication
is underwritten solely by

Inner Child Press International

Inner Child Press is a Publishing Company Founded and Operated by Writers. Our personal publishing experiences provides us an intimate understanding of the sometimes daunting challenges Writers, New and Seasoned may face in the Business of Publishing and Marketing their Creative "Written Work".

For more Information

Inner Child Press International

www.innerchildpress.com

~ fini ~

www.ingramcontent.com/pod-product-compliance
Lightning Source LLC
LaVergne TN
LVHW010055110826
845155LV00028B/355

* 9 7 8 1 9 5 2 0 8 1 3 1 6 *

www.ingramcontent.com/pod-product-compliance
Lightning Source LLC
LaVergne TN
LVHW020051110826
845155LV00021B/67

9781937630225